MW01002928

TOKYO
& BEYOND

AUBURN PUBLIC LIBRARY
749 EAST THACH AVENUE
AUBURN, AL 36830
(334) 501-3190

OCT 2019

Author
Anna Chittenden

Photographer
Anna Chittenden

Editing & Proofreading
Rebecca Dyer

Contributors
Frank Striegl
Stephanie Crohin
Kathryn Bagley
Danielle Demetriou

Designer
Sarah and Schooling

Map Illustrator
Rinanda Adelia

Cover Image
'Tsukimi-yu onsen, Shimotakaido'
by Stephanie Crohin

First Edition, 2019
Lost Guides
www.thelostguides.com

Copyright
© Lost Guides, 2019

All Rights Reserved.
No part of this publication may be reproduced, stored in a retrieval
system, or transmitted in any form or by any means, electronic,
mechanical, photocopying, recording or otherwise, without prior
written permission of the copyright owner.

All the views in this book are those of Lost Guides alone and are
independent and impartial. Lost Guides has taken all reasonable
care in preparing this book and makes no warranty regarding the
accuracy or completeness of the content. Certain details are subject
to change. Opening times may vary, and businesses can close.
Lost Guides cannot accept responsibility for any consequences
from the use of this book.

Printed and bound in Singapore by Markono Print Media Pte Ltd

MIX
Paper from
responsible sources
FSC
www.fsc.org
FSC™ C009578

ISBN 978-981-14-0538-9

Work with Lost Guides
Lost Guides is able to deliver bespoke travel guides and custom
content for your business in both print and digital formats. If you
like what we do, please email *hello@thelostguides.com*

Stock this book
If you are interested in stocking *Lost Guides - Tokyo & Beyond*, please
email *hello@thelostguides.com*

Also available in this series:
Lost Guides - Bali & Islands
Lost Guides - Singapore

TOKYO
& BEYOND

A UNIQUE, STYLISH AND OFFBEAT TRAVEL
GUIDE TO TOKYO & BEYOND

LOST GUIDES

1ST EDITION

ANNA CHITTENDEN

Contents

Author's Notes
8

About the Author
10

Need to Know
12

10 Days in Japan
14

48 Hours in Tokyo
16

Tokyo Hotels &
Accommodation
18

Tokyo

Shibuya, Daikanyama
& Ebisu
26

Nakameguro
46

Roppongi
62

Harajuku
76

Omotesando
90

Shimokitazawa
106

Shinjuku
120

Ginza & Tokyo
Station
134

Ueno & Ryogoku
148

Near Tokyo

Kyoto & Around

Hakuba, Karuizawa,
Hakone, Mount Fuji
160

Kyoto, Nara,
Mount Koya
178

Contributors

Tokyo's Tastiest Ramen
Frank Striegl
204

The Secret Sentos
of Tokyo
Stephanie Crohin
212

Japan Photo Journal
Kathryn Bagley
220

Tokyo Index
230

Behind the Scenes
234

My Tokyo & Beyond
Travel Notes
236

Acknowledgments
239

Japan

● Sapporo

Tokyo

Kyoto
●

Kyoto
●

NaRa
●

Mount Koya
●

Sea of
Japan

● Hakuba

● Karuizawa

Tokyo ●

Mount Fuji ●

Hakone ●

Pacific
Ocean

Author's Notes

Lost Guides – Tokyo & Beyond is the third book in my Lost Guides travel series. Over the last three years, I've spent more than two months in Tokyo and other areas of Japan researching for this book. Initial impressions of Tokyo from afar led me to believe the city would be chaotic, futuristic and alien, but I've found the opposite to be true. What I discovered is a city that is steeped in tradition, charm and kindness, from the almost overly polite service in restaurants and the delightful neighbourhoods filled with independent places to eat and shop, to immersive cultural customs like the Japanese art of bathing. Using Tokyo as a starting point, Japan is a joy to travel around with fast and easy trains.

What's in the guide?

This book highlights 111 wonderful places in Tokyo, as well as 40 special spots to explore outside the city – each one personally visited and recommended by me. Starting with the capital itself, the book features nine neighbourhoods with suggestions ranging from affordable sushi spots, cool coffee stands, flea markets selling vintage kimonos to secret open-air sentos to bathe in after a long day. A quick hop on the bullet train will whisk you away to polar-opposite scenes: try skiing in Hakuba and onsen-hopping in Hakone; explore the rich heritage of Kyoto and stay in a monastery in Mount Koya; and fall in love with Mount Fuji before heading back to Tokyo for late-night karaoke. In addition, there are mini guides revealing a ramen expert's 9 favourite ramen shops and a public bath ambassador's 9 most special sentos in Tokyo, plus a gorgeous Japan photo journal – all from Tokyo-based contributors.

How did I choose what would go in the book?

I know immediately when I've walked into a place if I've made a good discovery – it's a feeling that's hard to pinpoint – most often it's a new experience, a new mood. It can be a taste that I've never known before, or seeing something beautiful. I get excited about showing people unique Japanese experiences, whether that's taking a traditional flower-arranging class at *Sogetsu School of Ikebana* (p75), spending the afternoon enjoying an outdoor bath at *Maenohara Onsen Sayano Yudokoro* (p154), or having an excellent omakase sushi meal at *Taku* (p100). I have organised the book by neighbourhood to encourage you to explore these areas further once you're there, using my suggestions as a starting point. Outside of Tokyo, I wanted to highlight a variety of experiences, from glamping in the foothills of Mount Fuji to relaxing in a Zen garden in Kyoto. All the recommendations that appear in this book are here because I think they're great. I don't accept commissions or payments to feature places in this guide – I simply write about what I love.

Who is this book for?

I created this book for today's traveller: the stylish nomad with an interest in experience, rather than expense, and an eye for quality, design and authenticity. It is for those that don't require over-the-top extravagance, but can stretch beyond the budget of a backpacker – those in search of the special places in between.

About the Author

Hi, I'm Anna and I'm the author, photographer and explorer behind this book, *Lost Guides – Tokyo & Beyond*. You may have come across my previous books, but if you're new to them then hello! I'm originally from the UK and moved to Singapore in 2014, where I currently live. I love living in Asia and have made a beeline to Japan as much as possible since moving here. As an outsider, I'm always on the lookout for what is unique to each destination, be that food, art, culture, nature or everyday local life.

Lost Guides

I started my travel guide brand **Lost Guides** after becoming increasingly frustrated trying to find trustworthy and useful travel recommendations for someone like me, who is seeking authentic and unique experiences. I launched my website thelostguides.com with online guides and have published the books *Lost Guides – Bali and Islands* and *Lost Guides – Singapore*. *Lost Guides – Tokyo & Beyond* is my third book.

Say hello

I love to hear from my readers, and see what you get up to during your travels.

You can reach me via social media or by email:

- @lostguides
- @lostguides
- Lost Guides
- anna@thelostguides.com

Please share your lovely photos of your trip with me using the hashtag #lostguidestokyobeyond

www.thelostguides.com

Need to Know

Language:
In big cities like Tokyo and Kyoto, there is English signage at stations and tourist attractions, and increasingly restaurants are providing English menus. However, it is useful to learn some Japanese phrases (or bring a small phrase book with you) so that you can converse with locals.

Budget:
Japan is a fairly expensive country. The biggest cost for travellers is accommodation. Trains and taxis are pricey, although local public transport is reasonably priced. You don't need to spend much to get a great meal.

Transport:
Japan Rail Pass: If you plan to take multiple train journeys around Japan, it makes sense to buy a *Japan Rail Pass* (JR Pass). This allows unlimited travel on JR trains for one, two or three weeks. The pass can only be used by foreign tourists and you need to purchase one in your own country before travelling to Japan. A seven-day JR Pass costs ¥29,110.

Tokyo Metro: Taking the Metro is the easiest and quickest way to get around Tokyo. Buy a prepaid e-money card – there are two main ones, *Suica* and *Pasmo*. These cards can be used for Metro and bus travel as well as in convenience stores and some cafes and taxis.

Tokyo taxis: Taxis can be easily hailed on the street or at taxi ranks. Many only take cash (some take *Suica* and *Pasmo* cards). Have the destination address written in Japanese to show the driver.

Taxi apps:
- **JapanTaxi:** An easy to use, foreigner-friendly app with a payment function. Download the app before you go to Japan to activate it with a confirmation code. It's half the price of Uber.

- **Uber:** The company does operate in Tokyo, but it only offers big six-seater premium cars. It's the most expensive taxi option.

Money:

The currency in Japan is yen: ¥.

Cash: Japan is very much a cash-based country. Cash is still the preferred payment method for many restaurants, small shops and tourist attractions. Cash can be withdrawn at ATMs in convenience stores, such as 7-Eleven and Lawson.

Card: Hotels, high-end restaurants and shops take card.

Tipping: This is not expected in Japan.

Tax-free shopping: Many shops in Japan offer tax-free shopping for tourists. Bring your passport to the shop to receive 8% off purchases over ¥5,000.

SIM cards:

- Your time in Japan will be made infinitely easier with the use of a local SIM card with Internet data - especially for Google Maps, taxi apps and restaurant reservations.
- SIM cards are sold at the airport. Buy an unlimited data package: ¥4,980 for 8 days or ¥6,980 for 31 days.

When to go:

Japan has four distinct seasons, each offering a different experience:

- **Spring** (*March – May*) is a popular time to visit due to the cherry blossom season and mild weather.
- **Summer** (*June – Aug*) is very hot and humid in Japan – some might feel too hot, although this is the season for festivals and cultural celebrations.
- **Autumn** (*Sept – Nov*) has milder weather, although prone to typhoons in September. October is a good month to visit, especially for seeing the autumn colours.
- **Winter** (*Dec – Feb*) is a good time to visit if you want to enjoy winter sports and open-air onsens.

10 Days in Japan

Experience a bit of everything with
this slightly sped-up itinerary

Day 1-3
Tokyo – City & Sights

Treat yourself to a stay at **Hoshinoya Tokyo** (p22), an authentic modern ryokan. Visit Tsukiji Market (p146) for breakfast then wander through Hamarikyu Gardens (p145) for green tea and wagashi sweets in the teahouse. Head to Ginza to peruse the latest fashion at Dover Street Market (p143). Take the Ginza Line to Ueno and have lunch at **Inshotei** (p152) before exploring artefacts at nearby **Tokyo National Museum** (p153).

Day 4-5
Kyoto – Culture & Charm

Take the Shinkansen train from Tokyo to Kyoto. Stay at artisan-inspired hotel Malda Kyoto (p184). Visit the serene Tofukuji Temple (p194) and its Zen gardens. Head to Shugakuin Imperial Villa (p193) for a tour and afterwards taste 'takoyaki' - fried octopus balls at Takoyasu (p186).

Day 6
Nara – Temple Town

From Kyoto, take a day trip to Nara and see **Todai-ji Temple** (p197) and **Kofukuji National Treasure Museum** (p196). Stay in Osaka and eat okonomiyaki pancakes at **Hozenji Sanpei** (p199).

Day 7-8
Hakone – Hot Springs Village

Stay at the traditional ryokan hotel **Hakone Kamon** (p173) and wallow in the warm outdoor onsen baths. Then see stunning sculptures at **Hakone Open-Air Museum** (p174).

Day 9-10
Hakuba – Japanese Alps

Travel north of Tokyo to **Hakuba** (p164), near Nagano. Stay at **Phoenix Cocoon** (p167) and, if visiting in winter, ski in the Happo-one area in the Japanese Alps.

48 Hours in Tokyo

*The best way to spend two
days in the capital city*

Day 1

Stay at the stylish hotel **Claska** (p20) in Meguro. Walk or take a bus to the
Nakameguro neighbourhood. Have an exquisite Japanese lunch at **Higashiyama** (p54), browse collectable clothes at **J'antiques** (p59) and wander along
the Meguro River, grabbing a coffee from **Sidewalk Stand** (p51).

Walk to the Daikanyama neighbourhood. Explore the historical Kyu Asakura
House (p43) and grab a bite from Henry's Burger (p33) before browsing the
beautiful bookstore, Daikanyama T-Site (p41).

Come evening, head to the bright lights of Shibuya. Walk the Shibuya
Crossing (p45), have beers at Shibuya Nonbei Yokocho (p38) and go for
dinner at Hiroo Onogi (p36).

Day 2

Venture to the young and fun neighbourhood Shimokitazawa. Browse wonderful vintage shops like **Kalma** (p116) and **Haight & Ashbury** (p114). Take the train to **Japan Open-Air Folk House Museum** (p119) and discover old Japanese village houses.

Take the train to Shinjuku. Have lunch at **Standing Sushi Bar** (p124) and visit the **Samurai Museum** (p132). Relax in an onsen at **Thermae-Yu** (p130).

Head to Azabu-Juban for a tuna-topped pizza snack at Savoy (p68). See the city skyline lit up at night at Tokyo City View (p73). Have dinner at Shirosaka (p69) in Akasaka and afterwards do karaoke at Cote D'Azur (p74).

Tokyo Hotels & Accommodation

The hotel scene in Tokyo is catching up with that of other major cities and the requirements of the modern traveller. Previously, accommodation choices were limited to soulless business hotels or chains, and these options were overly expensive compared with those in similar cities. Today, there are a sprinkling of hotels infused with creativity and local charm. Depending on your budget and what sort of experiences you want to have, you can stay in an inexpensive capsule hotel, a mid-range minimalist design-hotel or a once-in-a-lifetime exquisite Japanese ryokan.

The Millennials Shibuya

🏠 1-20-13 Jinnan, Shibuya City

🚇 Shibuya

✈ themillennials.jp/shibuya

📷 @themillennials.shibuya

$ From ¥7,000

Sleeping in a capsule may traditionally be the preserve of drunken Japanese salarymen who've missed the last train home, but *The Millennials* has given compact sleeping a stylish, creative makeover. A welcome presence in neon-lit Shibuya (historically short on good places to stay), the hotel spans six floors and has 120 high-tech 'Smart Pods'. Reinvented for a new generation, they have reclining beds, Serta mattresses, an integrated iPod system and, in some cases, pull-down screens for private film viewings. A highlight? The 20 'Art Pods' on the 5th floor, decorated by a string of artists and designers who were given free rein. There are also spacious communal areas, such as co-working spaces and an outdoor terrace.

Muji Hotel Ginza

Muji Hotel Ginza (the first in Japan and the third globally) opened in April 2019 on the upper floors of the 10-storey flagship store in retail hub Ginza. Its 79 guestrooms resemble, perhaps unsurprisingly, a Muji catalogue. Despite varying sizes (there are nine different room types), they are unanimously serene, with warm oak, neutral fabrics and grey stone bathrooms. Best of all? You can buy everything just downstairs – from the navy pyjamas and the white kettle right down to the bed. Delicious Japanese-style breakfasts and regional cuisine are also served up in the stylishly simple restaurant *WA*.

🏠 3-3-5 Ginza, Chuo City

🚇 Ginza

↖ hotel.muji.com/ginza

 #mujihotel

💲 From ¥15,000

Nohga Hotel Ueno

🏠 2-21-10 Higashiueno, Taito City

🚇 Ueno

🏹 nohgahotel.com

📷 @nohgahotel.ueno

💲 From ¥18,000

Local design steals the show at *Nohga Hotel Ueno*, as befits its location in east Tokyo, an area famed for its craftsmanship heritage. Bespoke work by a string of local creatives is peppered throughout the 10-storey new-build, which is just a few minutes on foot from Ueno Station. Observe the details, such as the leather 'Do Not Disturb' signs hanging on the doors of the 130 guestrooms (made by design studio SyuRo); room keys (by generations-old family-crest company Studio Kyogen); and a fleet of 20 burgundy Tokyobikes for hire. The airy Lobby Lounge, filled with green plants and bespoke Stellar Works furniture, sits alongside *Bistro NOHGA*, where French-Japanese food is served up with natural wines.

Claska

🏠 1-3-18 Chuocho, Meguro City

🚇 Gakugei-daigaku or Meguro

🏹 claska.com

📷 @claska_tokyo

💲 From ¥25,000

Claska is Tokyo's original design hotel, the antithesis to the corporate offerings available at its time of opening in 2003. With only 20 rooms, this is a proper boutique hotel – small, friendly and warm. We stayed in room 503, one of its 'modern' category rooms, and at 38 square metres it felt incredibly spacious, with a huge bed, wide windows and a glass-walled bathroom. I really loved their shop *DO*, a lifestyle store selling cool curated Japanese crafts, clothing and homeware products. Do note that the location of *Claska* is slightly out of the way in the Meguro area, although you're not far from my favourite neighbourhood, Nakameguro.

Hyatt Centric Ginza

Hyatt Centric Ginza is a buzzing city hotel with an unbeatable location right in the heart of Ginza. Opened in 2018, the hotel was created with the modern traveller in mind in a building that was originally a newspaper printing press. The design feels contemporary but cosy, with comfy sofas and warm lighting in the lobby. The rooms are compact but well designed – out with drab business grey and in with brightly coloured walls, rugs and patterned cushions, with details such as Bose speakers, Nespresso coffee machines and yukata robes. The breakfast at its restaurant *NAMIKI667* is fabulous.

6-6-7 Ginza, Chuo City

Ginza

hyatt.com

@hyattcentricginza

From ¥45,000

Hoshinoya Tokyo

🏠 1-9-1 Otemachi,
Chiyoda City

🚇 Otemachi or
Tokyo Station

↖ hoshinoya.com/tokyo

⊙ @hoshinoya.official

$ From ¥75,000

At the top end of the scale is *Hoshinoya Tokyo*, the pinnacle of Japanese elegance and hospitality. Designed by architect Rie Azuma and opened in 2016, the hotel is a modern take on the traditional ryokan. Rooms are spacious and serene, with shoji sliding doors, an enormous futon bed and a bathroom that could be a spa. There's a wonderful onsen on the rooftop, with a bath gloriously open to the elements that uses hot spring water drawn from 1,500m below ground. For dinner, descend to the basement to a cave-like Zen garden space, where you are served 'Nippon cuisine', food prepared within a culinary philosophy that focuses on fish. Enjoy cultural experiences, such as a Japanese tea ceremony and watch a grand kagura performance (Japanese magic trick show) in the sake lounge.

Airbnb

In theory, renting a local's apartment in a hip area of Tokyo sounds ideal. But *Airbnb* took a dive when, in 2018, the supply of listings was wiped out after new laws for 'minpaku' – private accommodation rentals – were introduced. There are still a few good listings, but you'll need to book well in advance. Convenient and fun areas to stay are around Shibuya, Nakameguro and Omotesando. We liked this modern Japanese-style apartment in Akasaka, near Roppongi. It has a separate tatami living room, a kitchen-diner and a big bathroom, and is within walking distance to Metro stations and sights.

🏠 2-20-15, Akasaka, Minato City

🚇 Akasaka

🢔 airbnb.com/rooms/27715692

💲 From ¥30,000

Tokyo

Shinjuku

Shinjuku National Garden

Yoyogi Park

Harajuku

Omotesando

Roppongi

Shimokitazawa

Shibuya

Nakameguro

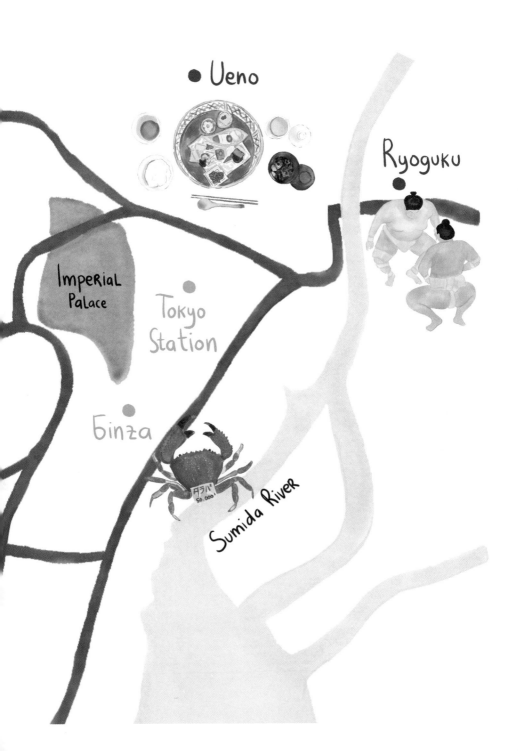

Shibuya, Daikanyama & Ebisu

Bright Lights & Elegant Enclaves

For a first-time visitor to Tokyo, **Shibuya** is one of the first ports of call. This is the Tokyo of your imagination: busy and bustling, with bright neon lights adorning every surface in sight. Think of it as Tokyo's version of Times Square. Shibuya Station is one of the busiest in the world, with a flood of people spilling out onto the streets and over the famous Shibuya Crossing.

As the vibrant centre of youth culture, there's always something going on at any time of the day. Wander down streets filled with the latest fashion boutiques and squeeze into tiny stand-up bars come evening.

But as soon as you stroll slightly south of Shibuya, this madness dissolves to gentler adjoining neighbourhoods, elegant **Daikanyama** and laid-back **Ebisu**. Daikanyama feels quiet but considered, with tree-lined avenues dotted with sophisticated shops and smart restaurants. A five-minute walk away and you're in Ebisu, a similarly refined neighbourhood that's also known for its great late-night ramen shops.

When you plan your route, bear in mind that Tokyo is a great walking city, where you can meander easily from one neighbourhood to the next, enjoying a wonderful contrast of sensory experiences between each area.

SHIBUYA, Daikanyama & Ebisu

③ The Millenials
Shibuya

⑪

⑭

⑰

Uoriki Kaisen Sushi

④

Shibuya

⑥

⑦

Tamagawa-Dori Ave

⑨

Daikanyama T-Site

⑬

Daikanyama

②

⑮

⑤

to Nakameguro

to HaRaJuku

Shibuya Nonbei Yokocho

to Omotesando

10

16

Roppongi - DoRi Ave

AFuRi

Ebisu

Meiji - DoRi Ave

1

12

8

Afuri

1 *Tasty Tsukemen*

Afuri is my go-to spot for quick, easy and tasty ramen in Tokyo. My first *Afuri* experience was in its original Ebisu branch, which opened in 2003, an unassuming narrow restaurant with 20 counter seats facing the open kitchen. I went for its 'yuzu tsukemen', a cold ramen with dry noodles that are plunged into a delicious dipping sauce before each mouthful, flavoured with zesty 'yuzu' (a Japanese citrus fruit). *Afuri* now has branches conveniently dotted around Tokyo near Metro stations in Nakameguro, Azabu-Juban, Roppongi and Shinjuku. It's open from 11am to 5am, so great for midnight munchies!

🏠 117 Building 1F, Ebisu, Shibuya City

🚇 Ebisu

🏹 afuri.com

📷 @afuri_official

🕐 Mon – Sun 11am – 5am

🔔 Walk-in

💲 ¥1,060

2 Shuichi

Shuichi is a super-local, blink-and-you'll-miss-it ramen restaurant occupying a basement on a quiet road in Ebisu, which was shown to me by Frank from '5am Ramen' (who I subsequently asked to write 'Tokyo's Tastiest Ramen' on p204). *Shuichi* specialises in curry ramen and, honestly, offers one of the most umami dishes I've tried – especially comforting on a cold winter's night. The union of ramen and curry is a whole new flavour experience to enjoy.

🏠 92 Yama Building, B1F, Ebisu-Nishi, Shibuya City

🚇 Ebisu

🕐 Mon – Sat 11am – 5am, Sun 11am – 11pm

🔔 Walk-in

$ ¥980

3 Menya Nukaji

If you're looking for a solid ramen shop for a tasty pitstop while pounding the pavements around Shibuya, then *Menya Nukaji* is the place to go. Located down quiet Kuyakusho Street, not far from *Muji*, it's a small and welcoming space with seats for only seven or so diners. Run by a friendly ramen-enthused husband-and-wife team, it specialises in both ramen and tsukemen.

🏠 3-12, 1F Udagawacho, Shibuya City

🚇 Shibuya

📷 @menya_nukaji

🕐 Mon – Fri 11am – 4pm and 6pm – 8pm, Sat 11am – 4pm, Closed Sun

🔔 Walk-in

$ ¥980

Uoriki Kaisen Sushi

4 *Speedy Sushi in Shibuya*

Uoriki Kaisen Sushi is a casual and affordable place for sushi, conveniently situated in Shibuya Station, and a good choice for an easy lunch in the area. It's essentially a restaurant in a supermarket, located in basement 1 of the food hall section of Tokyu Department Store, called 'Tokyu Food Show'. It can be hard to find, so look out for the indigo-blue curtains with a white and orange logo. We went for the 'omakase nigiri' option, which is an eight-piece sushi set for the very reasonable price of ¥1,200. Enjoy bites of horse mackerel, salted salmon roe, scallop and tasty tuna, with a warming side of clam-filled miso soup.

🏠 B1, Tokyu Department Store, 2-24-1 Shibuya City

🚇 Shibuya

↖ uoriki.co.jp

⊘ Mon – Sun 10am – 9pm

🔔 Walk-in

Ⓢ ¥1,200

Henry's Burger

5 *Brilliant Burgers*

Yes, I like to eat American-style hamburgers in Japan – especially when they are as good as what's on offer at *Henry's Burger* in Daikanyama. I would describe *Henry's* as 'fancy fast food'; the burgers come quickly but are very high-quality and made with 100% kuroge wagyu beef, with each cow chosen by chef and 'beef craftsman' Kentaro Nakahara (who went by the name Henry while living in California). With only four seats in a casual take-away-style setting, *Henry's* is best suited for when you want a tasty bite on the go. A single patty burger starts at ¥860 and the combo with fries and drink is ¥1,180.

🏠 1-36-6 Ebisu-Nishi, Shibuya City

🚈 Daikanyama

📍 henrysburger.com

📷 @henrysburgerdaikanyama

🕑 Mon – Sun 11am – 8pm

🔔 Walk-in

💲 ¥860

Kaikaya by the Sea

6 *Seafood & Sake*

We were taken to *Kaikaya* by some Japanese friends during our first trip to Tokyo. It's a fun, laid-back 'izakaya', essentially a casual pub-style restaurant where both food and alcohol flow freely. As the name suggests this is a seafood restaurant, so expect lots of sashimi and grilled fish. Be sure to try the house special 'tuna sparerib' – melt-in-your-mouth marinated tuna jaw. If you're feeling adventurous, try the 'shirako' – cod sperm, served baked in gorgonzola gratin (which our friends surprised us with). *Kaikaya's* eight-course set menu is good value at ¥3,500 and includes fish carpaccio, sashimi, tuna sparerib and cherry-blossom gelato. This is also a great spot if you're travelling as a group, with spacious seating and a lively atmosphere.

🏠 23-7 Maruyama-cho, Shibuya City

🚇 Shibuya

☎ +81 337700878

🏹 kaikaya.com

📷 #kaikayabythesea

🕐 Mon – Sun 5.30pm – 11.30pm

🔔 Reservation through OpenTable

💲 ¥3,500

Cignale Enoteca

7 *Intimate Italian*

A friend who moved to Tokyo spent months trying to get a table at Italian-Japanese restaurant *Cignale Enoteca*, and we were the lucky recipients of such perseverance! Hidden down a back-alley a mile or so from Shibuya, *Cignale Enoteca* is a tiny 10-seater restaurant bursting with character and charm. Flickering light is provided by antique silver candleholders, propped on the wooden countertop next to baskets of freshly made pasta and trays of vegetables ready to be cooked. Chef Toshiji Tomori will personally serve you up an eight-course omakase menu with a delightful variety of dishes, all decided by what produce is in season and at its best that day.

🏠 1-5-11 Komaba, Meguro City

🚈 Shibuya

☎ +81 334857371

↖ cignale.jp

📷 @cignale_enoteca

🕐 Mon – Sat 6pm – 12am, Closed Sun

🔔 Reservation through website

Ⓢ ¥15,000

Hiroo Onogi

8 *Modern Japanese Omakase*

Hiroo Onogi is located in Hiroo, an upmarket neighbourhood nestled between Ebisu and Roppongi. The restaurant is sophisticated but fun, with lively chefs serving contemporary Japanese food, and is easily one of my top picks for dinner in Tokyo. It has an extensive à la carte menu – from deep-fried Iwate oysters to beef rump steak from Gunma – or you can go for the omakase menu, which starts from ¥9,500. With a focus on fish, I loved the sea urchin, assorted sashimi and signature lobster pot rice. Ask for counter seats for a front-row view of the chefs at work.

🏠 Barbizon 22-2F, 5-8-11 Hiroo, Shibuya City

🚇 Hiroo

☎ +81 364477657

🏹 discovery-t.com/hiroo-onogi

📷 @hiroo_onogi

🕐 Mon – Sat 6pm – 12pm, Closed Sun

🔔 Reservation by email: hiroo-onogi@discovery-t.com

💲 ¥9,500

Falò

9 *Bonfire Bites*

Falò is one of those relaxed neighbourhood restaurants that feels both laid-back and carefully thought out. Its hidden location in a basement in trendy Daikanyama makes the space feel like a secret lair, with the wood-chipped walls and ceiling creating a cosy cave-like feel. 'Falò' is the Italian word for bonfire, and the restaurant's focal point is the red-hot charcoal fire in the centre of the space. This Japanese-style Italian restaurant specialises in grilled meats, such as duck, wild boar and venison, as well as the most perfect pasta, such as classic carbonara and spaghetti with sea urchin sauce. The Italian wines are really good and it's open on a Sunday (when many restaurants are closed).

🏠 10 Luz Daikanyama B1, Daikanyama-cho, Shibuya City

🚃 Daikanyama

☎ +81 364550206

🏹 falo-daikanyama.com

📷 @falo_daikanyama

🕐 Mon – Sat 6pm – 11.30pm, Sun 3pm – 9pm, Closed Thurs

🔔 Reservation through website

💲 ¥5,000

Shibuya Nonbei Yokocho

10 *Drunkards' Alley*

Who would have thought that a stone's throw from sleek Shibuya Station you could find a traditional 'yokocho', an old-school alleyway jam-packed with miniature bars that originally sprung up in the 1950s? *Shibuya Nonbei Yokocho*, widely known as 'Drunkards' Alley', is made up of around 40 ramshackle miniature bars, seating as few as four people. The area maintains a nostalgic charm, with the narrow walkway faintly lit by red lanterns. It's a great spot to stop for a few Sapporo beers before dinner in Shibuya (I wouldn't eat here), with a quirky and friendly vibe.

🏠 1-25 Shibuya, Shibuya City

🚇 Shibuya

🕐 Evening

🔔 Walk-in

Muji

11 *Minimalist Lifestyle Supplies*

Muji was the only place I wanted to get my back-to-school stationery from, and I still use the denim pencil case I bought there 20 years ago. Yes, they have shops all over the world, but a *Muji*-lover like me has to visit one of their big stores in Tokyo. Shibuya isn't the biggest branch, but I prefer this one for its good location and variety. As well as its usual ranges, look out for *Muji's* ongoing collaboration with design brand IDÉE, selling colourful lifestyle items from linen dresses to plant pots. Stop for lunch at *Café & Meal Muji*, with delicious lunch sets from ¥850.

🏠 21-1 Shibuya Seibu, Udagawacho, Shibuya City

🚉 Shibuya

🏹 muji.com

⌾ @muji_global

⦸ Mon – Sun 10am – 9pm

Tokyo Edo Miso

12 *Miso Paste Parlour*

🏠 5-1-30 Hiroo, Shibuya City

🚇 Hiroo

🏹 edomiso.jp

⊘ Mon – Fri 11am – 5pm,
Closed Sat – Sun

The one item I always bring back in my suitcase from Tokyo is a pot of miso paste from *Tokyo Edo Miso*. Established in 1919, this gorgeous little shop is as authentic as you can get. It solely sells miso paste, which you can sample in diluted miso shots. They sell different types: Edo miso, Edo sweet miso, country miso and Sendai miso, which you can buy in increments of 100g. A 200g pot of miso is around ¥850. Use it in your cooking as a salt alternative, adding a deep rich flavour to homemade meals.

Daikanyama T-Site

13 *Beautiful Bookstore*

Often hailed as one of the world's most beautiful bookshops, *Daikanyama T-Site* is a whimsical store based around the theme of 'a library in the woods' and has won many design awards since it opened in 2011. Its spacious size and unique design by Tokyo architecture firm Klein Dytham has made it something of a landmark in the Daikanyama neighbourhood, and in Tokyo itself. The store is laid out over three different buildings, with smaller rooms and cafes creating a cosy atmosphere in which to enjoy browsing books, as well as indie and offbeat magazines in both Japanese and English.

🏠 16-15 Sarugakucho, Shibuya City

🚇 Daikanyama

🔖 real.tsite.jp/daikanyama

📷 @daikanyama.tsutaya

🕐 Mon – Sun 7am – 2am

Disk Union

14 *Vintage Vinyl*

Vinyl is officially making its way back into the lives of modern music lovers, with nearly 10 million vinyl albums sold in 2018 in the US alone. Tokyo has a great choice of used record shops, and my DJ friend Krish pointed me in the direction of *Disk Union*. Conveniently situated five minutes' walk from Shibuya Station, it's honestly worth a visit solely for the beautiful album artwork. Discover mint-condition David Bowie, Rolling Stones, Eric Clapton and Elvis records, with jazz, soul and reggae on the lower floor. There is also a *Disk Union* megastore in Shinjuku and a nice small one in Shimokitazawa.

🏠 Antenna 21-2F/3F, 30-7 Udagawacho, Shibuya City

🚇 Shibuya

↖ diskunion.net

📷 @diskunion

🕐 Mon – Sun 11am – 9pm

Kyu Asakura House

15 *Historical House*

Kyu Asakura House is a wonderful time capsule of forgotten early 20th-century Tokyo, nestled discreetly behind an unassuming rustic bamboo gate in the Daikanyama neighbourhood. Built in 1919 as the private home of politician Torajiro Asakura, this house is a stunning example of Taisho-era architecture and classified as an Important Cultural Property, having remarkably survived earthquakes, fires and wars that destroyed much of the city. For a small entry fee of ¥100, you can wander around the beautifully conserved rooms in this two-storey wooden house. See the Japanese cedar room, an inward-facing zashiki room, a Western-style room and a tearoom, as well as a glorious garden. There are few other visitors here, making it a very Zen-like experience.

🏠 29-20 Sarugakucho, Shibuya City

🚉 Daikanyama

🕐 Tues – Sun 10am – 4.30pm, Closed Mon

💲 ¥100

Nanzuka

16 *Underground Art Gallery*

Nanzuka is a cool contemporary art gallery hidden behind a nondescript black door five minutes' walk from Shibuya Station, and is absolutely worth popping into. Occupying a spacious basement space, the gallery shows the work of new and exciting artists, with about eight exhibitions per year. Shows are fairly small, so you won't need long to browse the artworks, and entry is free. The gallery also represents notable artists such as the colourful works of Keiichi Tanaami, the girls of Harumi Yamaguchi and the charcoal-and-ink drawings of Hiroki Tsukuda (who was exhibiting when I visited).

🏠 2-17-3 Shibuya Ibis Building B2F, Shibuya City

🚌 Shibuya

🔾 nug.jp

📷 @nanzukaunderground

🕑 Tues – Sat 11am – 7pm, Closed Sun - Mon

Ⓢ Free

Shibuya Crossing

17 *Crazy Crossroads*

🏠 Exit 8 (Hachiko Exit) of
Shibuya Station

🚇 Shibuya

Nothing says Tokyo more than a walk across *Shibuya Crossing*, famous for being one of the busiest intersections in the world, with thousands of people crossing at a time. The area around Shibuya Station comes alive at night, with towering neon billboards and the bright lights of buildings illuminating the sky. While walking across *Shibuya Crossing*, you can feel the surge of energy and the area's vibrant atmosphere. Afterwards, go up to Starbucks in Tsutaya to see the iconic crossing from above.

Nakameguro

Relaxed Riverside Retreat

I have to admit it: **Nakameguro** is my favourite of all of Tokyo's neighbourhoods. Maybe it's the delightful walk along the banks of the Meguro River, lined with creative shops and sweet cafes, where you can spot the most stylish of Tokyoites out walking their dogs on the weekends.

Or it could be the charming back roads that feel truly local, with their sprinkling of superb coffee stands and intriguing vintage shops. It could also be the fabulous food, from a best-in-class pizza joint to restaurants serving meticulous modern Japanese cuisine.

The area feels relaxed, but at the same time there's always something new and interesting to discover down a narrow alley. Nakameguro is on the one hand suburban – a low-rise area that doesn't feel at all like you're in one of the world's most busy and populated cities – but, on the other hand, it's a mere 25-minute stroll to Shibuya Station. The area attracts artists and creatives, who live and work here, creating a vibrant, inspiring atmosphere.

Nakameguro

Golden Brown

Higashi-yama

Yamate-Dori Ave

4

6

9

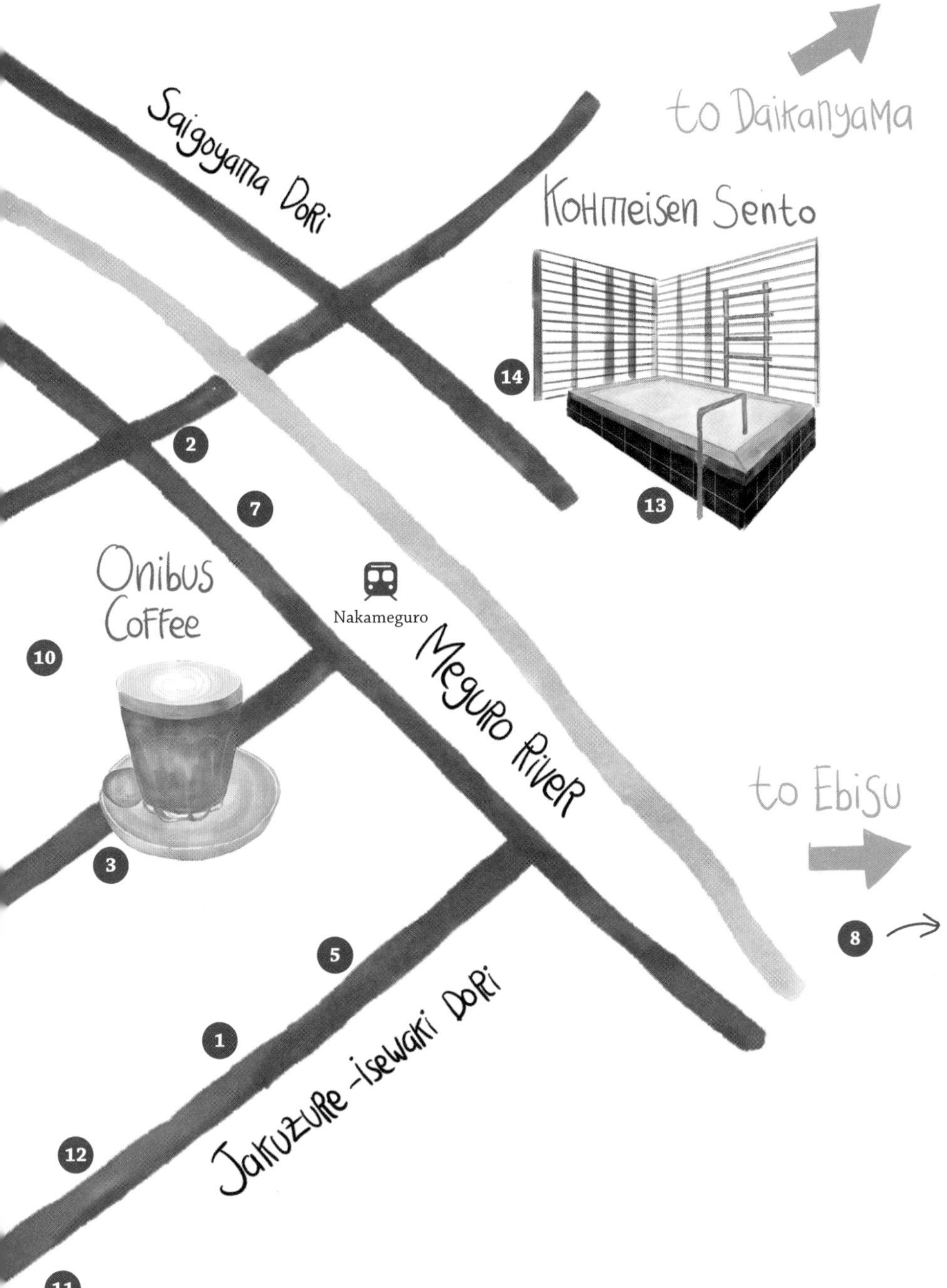

Saigoyama Dori

to Daikanyama

Kohmeisen Sento

14

13

2

7

Onibus
Coffee

Nakameguro

Meguro River

10

3

to Ebisu

5

8 →

1

12

Jakuzure -isewaki Dori

11

Trasparente

1 *Glorious Baked Goods*

I have a soft spot for brilliant bakeries and often make it my mission to hunt down the best one in the neighbourhood. *Trasparente* is situated down a delightful street in Kamimeguro with a lovely local vibe, where you'll find quirky shops like *J'antiques*, old bookshops and hardware stores. It makes everything in-house and you can see the busy bakers freshly making bread and pastries throughout the day. If I'm staying in Nakameguro, I'll come here for breakfast most mornings! I absolutely love the white chocolate and the fruit-filled pastries. They also do a nice chai latte.

🏠 FD Building 1F, 2-12-11 Kamimeguro, Meguro City

🚇 Nakameguro

🏹 trasparente.info

📷 @trasparente_2008

🕐 Wed – Mon 9am – 7pm, Closed Tues

🔔 Walk-in

💲 ¥800

② Sidewalk Stand

At the weekends it's wonderful to walk along the river in Nakameguro, browsing the cool vintage and independent shops that line the canal. If you fancy a coffee, pop into *Sidewalk Stand*, a small stand-up coffee shop with a handful of bar stools, both indoors and outside. It's a great spot for people watching and also sells craft beer and gooey grilled sandwiches.

🏠 Saito Building, 1-23-14, Aobadai, Meguro City

🚇 Nakameguro

↖ sidewalk.jp

📷 @sidewalk_stand

🕐 Mon – Sun 9am – 9pm

💲 ¥480

③ Onibus Coffee

Hidden down a backstreet near Nakameguro Station, *Onibus Coffee* is a quirky, sand-coloured coffee hut that is clearly a meeting place for young, trendy locals. Catering to the neighbourhood's creative crowd, this specialty coffee house roasts its own beans on site, and you can see the goings-on in the small roaster out back. It sells regular espresso and latte, as well as hand-drip filter coffee.

🏠 2-14-1 Kamimeguro, Meguro City

🚇 Nakameguro

↖ onibuscoffee.com

📷 @onibuscoffee

🕐 Mon – Sun 9am – 6pm

💲 ¥400

Golden Brown

4 *Retro Burger Bar*

This might sound strange, but a burger from *Golden Brown* was one of my first meals in Tokyo! We'd been to a traditional wedding the night before (with courses of delicate Japanese food), so were seeking something comforting and stodgy the morning after. *Golden Brown* is a 15-seater restaurant with a 1950s American diner vibe. It serves Coca-Cola in glass bottles and features old-fashioned hand-painted gold signage on the window by local artist Nuts. I always go for the avocado and cheese burger with fries, and I love the way it's served in a practical white paper sleeve.

🏠 2-3-1 Higashiyama, Meguro City

🚇 Nakameguro

↖ goldenbrown.info

📷 @goldenbrown_official

⊘ Mon – Sun 11.30am – 10pm

🔔 Walk-in

$ ¥1,500

Seirinkan

5 *Perfect Pizzas*

🏠 2-6-4 Kamimeguro,
Meguro City

🚆 Nakameguro

☎ +81 337145160

🏹 theseirinkan.com

📷 #seirinkan

🕐 Mon – Fri 11.30am – 1.30pm
and 6pm – 8.45pm,
Sat – Sun 11.30am – 2.30pm
and 5pm – 8.45pm

🔔 Walk-in or reservation by phone

💲 ¥1,500

Burgers, pizzas, doughnuts – yes, Tokyo loves to take foreign food and put a Japanese spin on it (read: make it flawless). *Seirinkan* serves simple Neapolitan-style pizza and is best known for featuring on the Netflix show 'Ugly Delicious'. It offers just two types of pizza: margherita and marinara (tomato sauce, no cheese) at ¥1,500 a pizza. In addition, *Seirinkan* has seriously good starters, such as caprese salad and burrata. When entering the tall, lofty restaurant, you are greeted with a blazing pizza oven, where chef Kakinuma – one of the original pizza masters – works his magic. For solo diners, there are counter seats at the bar, as well as two floors of group seating.

Higashi-yama

6 *Contemporary Japanese Cuisine*

More than a meal, *Higashi-yama* is a quintessential Japanese experience. You should never choose a restaurant based on looks alone, but *Higashi-yama* is as inspiring for its blend of traditional and modern interior design as it is for its wonderful, thoughtful food. Located in a beautiful house in the heart of Nakameguro, it serves home-style modern Japanese food and is amazing value. For ¥3,500, enjoy a seasonal lunch set with a stunning selection of eight appetisers – little snacks like tofu, pumpkin, amberjack, mushroom and crab – followed by fish or tempura, then desserts, plus matcha tea, all served in gorgeous ceramics.

🏠 1-21-25 Higashiyama, Meguro City

🚇 Nakameguro

☎ +81 357201300

↖ higashiyama-tokyo.jp

⊙ @higashiyama_tokyo

🕐 Tues – Sat 11.30am – 3pm and 6pm – 12am, Mon 6pm – 12am, Closed Sun

🔔 Walk-in or reservation through website or by phone

$ ¥3,500

KushiWakaMaru

7 *Casual Chicken Skewers*

KushiWakaMaru is a fun, laid-back restaurant attracting a young and local crowd. It serves yakitori, a popular Japanese cuisine in which different parts of a chicken are skewered and grilled over a red-hot charcoal fire. It's a bustling izakaya–style establishment that's good for groups, so come with friends for dinner and share plates of tsukune (chicken meatballs), wings and chicken skin. *KushiWakaMaru* also does veggie skewers, such as eggplant, and its special, pepper stuffed with cheese. And it has a good selection of sake. It doesn't take reservations, so just turn up, write down your name and wait a short while for a seat. Casual and unpretentious with a lively atmosphere – this isn't fine dining!

🏠 1-19-2 Kamimeguro, Meguro City

🚇 Nakameguro

↖ kushiwakamaru.com

📷 #kushiwakamaru

🕐 Mon – Sun 5pm – 12am

🔔 Walk-in

💲 ¥4,000

Tonkatsu Tonki

8 *Pork Cutlet Counter*

Tonkatsu Tonki is something of an institution, serving tonkatsu – deep-fried pork cutlet covered with breadcrumbs (similar to European schnitzel) – since 1939. There are only two options here: 'hire-katsu' with lean meat or 'rohsu' with fatty pork, both ¥1,900 each and coming with rice, miso soup, cabbage, pickles and tea. *Tonki* opens at 4pm, but get there at 3.50pm before a queue starts to form. There are about 30 or so counter seats so you'll likely get seated immediately. I love the old-school set-up with its traditional wood flooring and the quick, professional service. *Tonkatsu Tonki* is right by Meguro Station, six stops on the bus from Nakameguro Station.

🏠 1-1-2 Shimomeguro, Meguro City

🚇 Meguro

📷 @tonkatsu_tonki

🕐 Wed – Mon 4pm – 10.45pm, Closed Tues

🔔 Walk-in

💲 ¥1,900

85 / Hachigo

9 *Fermentation Focused*

There's a row of cool little businesses, restaurants and shops nestled in the arches under the railway track from Nakameguro Station towards Yutenji. Among other curious finds is the 'fermentation-focused' *85 / Hachigo*, an interestingly curated shop that sells items such as jars of colourful pickles, natural soy sauces and craft miso paste from Kanagawa. As well as food supplies, it sells useful home items that support a healthy environment. I also love its range of artisanal glassware and ceramics.

🏠 Nakame Gallery Street, 2-45-12, Kamimeguro, Meguro City

🚈 Nakameguro

🔗 85life.jp

📷 @85life.jp

🕐 Mon – Sun 11am – 9pm

Traveler's Factory

10 *Explorers' Objects*

🏠 3-13-10 Kamimeguro,
Meguro City

🚇 Nakameguro

↖ travelers-factory.com

📷 @travelers_factory

🕐 Wed – Mon 12pm – 8pm,
Closed Tues

Home of the Traveler's Notebook, the much-loved journal, *Traveler's Factory* is a cute but iconic little stationery shop in a somewhat residential part of Nakameguro, although not far from the station. The store is filled with vintage leather-bound travel journals, travel tags, stickers and general travel-inspired goodies. Its 1950s-style airline memorabilia, stamps and diaries give a nod to the bygone era of travel. The store itself is small and charming, and was formerly used as a paper-processing factory. *Traveler's Factory* also has stores at Tokyo Station and the airport, but this is the original with its own authentic appeal.

J'antiques

11 *Americana Attire*

When shopping, I much prefer to buy secondhand and vintage clothing (fun fact: I used to run a small vintage clothing business in the UK!). When stepping into *J'antiques*, it feels like you've entered an old attic in America's Midwest. Find racks of dirty denim overalls, worn-in leather cowboy boots, original Levi's rodeo shirts, lumberjack belts and even dishcloths. The pieces are like collector's items or costumes, which is reflected in the higher pricing than other vintage shops. I love this shop's deep dedication to true Americana.

🏠 2-25-13, Kamimeguro, Meguro City

🚇 Nakameguro

📷 @uchidahitoshi

🕐 Mon – Sun 12pm – 9pm

12 Konguri

Konguri is a fun little antique shop opposite *J'antiques* - it's the one with the pink-and-green Fujicolor sign. *Konguri* sells original items for the home, such as blue translucent apothecary bottles, vintage ceramics and glasses, and Japanese block prints (which could be used to make the coolest paper!). Prices are good value too.

🏠 2-44-5 Kamimeguro, Meguro

🚇 Nakameguro

📷 @konguri_antique

🕐 Mon – Sun 1pm – 9pm

13 Toll Free

You'll find *Toll Free* on a road behind Nakameguro Station, along with some other nice vintage shops. It mainly sells American workwear and, while stock can feel more catered to men, has groovy tie-dye T-shirts, cheapish Burberry trench coats and retro Adidas tracksuits.

🏠 1-6-5 Kamimeguro, Meguro City

🚇 Nakameguro

📷 @toll_free_official

🕐 Mon – Sun 11am – 9pm

Kohmeisen Sento

14 *Rooftop Bath*

While reading this book, you'll soon grasp my obsession with Japanese public baths, known as 'sentos' or 'onsens'. I try to visit a sento every day when in Japan, normally at around 5pm, when I'm tired of walking around all day and before the evening's activities. Sentos are like luxurious spas, but with a tiny price tag of around ¥400 (slightly more if you need to hire a towel and soap). Located conveniently near Nakameguro Station, *Kohmeisen* has an amazing rooftop rotenburo (outside bath) made of wood, and is open to men and women separately on alternate weeks (it switches every Friday). While soaking in the rotenburo, you can hear trains rushing past while you relax under the dark sky – bliss!

 1-6-1 Kamimeguro, Meguro City

 Nakameguro

 kohmeisen.com

 Mon – Sun 3pm – 1am

$ ¥480

Roppongi

Lively & Raucous Region

Roppongi doesn't have the best reputation, as far as Tokyo's neighbourhoods go. The area has typically been associated with sleaze and all-night drinking, thus attracting the wrong sort of badly behaved tourist. The reality is that Roppongi is a bit of fun if you're looking for some nightlife or fancy belting out some tunes during a late-night karaoke session.

It's also a great place to see some amazing art, with the architectural delight *21_21 Design Sight* at Tokyo Midtown just a 20-minute walk from *Mori Art Museum* at Roppongi Hills, which adjoins *Tokyo City View* with its spectacular panoramic views of the city – best experienced at night.

Adjacent to Roppongi is the relaxed residential neighbourhood Azabu-Juban, an area that feels traditional and old-school, with a mix of well-to-do locals and expats calling it home. Come August, the streets host thousands of people dressed in yukata and brandishing fans at 'Azabu-Juban Noryo Matsuri', one of Tokyo's famous summer festivals.

Roppongi

Sogetsu School of Ikebana

12

9

Cote D'Azur

Roppongi

11

10

to Omotesando

8

2

Akasaka St

Akasaka

①

Shirosaka

⑥

Roppongi-Doki Ave

⑦

Azabu-Doki Ave

to Ginza
➡

Savoy

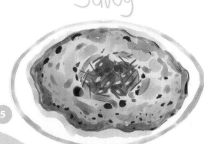

Azabu-Juban

③

④

⑤

① Sushi No Midori

When I first visited Tokyo and asked around for a good, affordable sushi lunch spot, *Midori* was the name that consistently came up. I went to the Akasaka branch, but they also have outlets in Ginza and Shibuya. It opens at 11am and I suggest getting there basically after breakfast, around 10.30am, to join the queue. I went for the ¥2,000 meal, which was absolutely huge, with tasty morsels of tuna, uni, ikura and unagi sushi, to name a few.

🏠 2F Akasaka Biz Tower, 5-3-1 Akasaka, Minato City

🚇 Akasaka

📍 sushinomidori.co.jp

📷 #sushinomidori

🕐 Mon – Sat 11am – 10pm, Sun 11am – 9pm

🔔 Walk-in

💲 ¥2,000

② Abe

Another great affordable sushi spot in Roppongi, *Abe* is less well known than *Midori*, and therefore much less busy when I popped in for a quick bite before a flight. Lunch sets start at the bargain price of ¥1,100, which included ten big pieces of sushi, miso soup and tea. The place is stylish and authentic – a perfect choice for lunch in the neighbourhood.

🏠 3-16-26 Halifax Building, Roppongi, Minato City

🚇 Roppongi

📷 #abesushi

🕐 Mon – Sun 11.30am – 2.30pm, 5.30pm – 5am

🔔 Walk-in

💲 ¥1,100

③ Nico Donuts

While staying with a friend in the Azabu-Juban area, I walked past *Nico* every day on the way to the Metro and could never resist stopping off to pick up one or two 'healthier' (I told myself!) treats. As they're made with soy paste and millet grains, they're much lighter and less greasy than usual doughnuts. *Nico* is a purely take-away shop that makes its produce on site, with flavours such as berry berry, white pistachio and maple nuts.

🏠 1-7-9 Azabujuban, Minato City

🚇 Azabu-Juban

📷 #nicodonuts

🕐 Mon – Sun 11am – 7.30pm

💲 ¥200

④ Naniwaya Sohonten

If you're looking for a more local treat, try 'taiyaki', a Japanese fish-shaped snack made from thin and crispy batter filled with red bean paste. Near Azabu-Juban Station, *Naniwaya Sohonten* is one of the oldest taiyaki spots in Tokyo, setting up shop in 1909, and this place still feels very traditional. Watch the masters at work filling the fish-shaped moulds and grilling the snack in front of you.

🏠 1-8-14 Azabu-Juban, Minato City

🚇 Azabu-Juban

📷 #naniwaya

🕐 Wed – Mon 10am-8pm, Closed Tues

💲 ¥180

Savoy

5 *Tasty Tuna Pizza*

It's almost worth making the pilgrimage to Tokyo for the pizza alone. Consider *Savoy*, opened in 1995, which takes original Naples-style pizza and gives it a remarkable Japanese twist in the form of tuna-topped goodness, aka 'Pizza Y'. The owner also runs the sushi restaurant below, hence the unique culinary collaboration. Be sure to visit this exact Savoy location, made famous by Netflix's 'Ugly Delicious', to try the tasty tuna variety. The restaurant is called *Savoy Tomato-to-Cheese* on Google – don't confuse it with the other *Savoy* branch, also in Azabu-Juban!

🏠 3-3-13 Azabujuban, Minato City

🚇 Azabu-Juban

🏹 savoy.vc

📷 #savoypizza

🕐 Thurs – Tues 12 – 2pm, 6pm –10pm, Closed Wed

🔔 Walk-in

💲 ¥1,500

Shirosaka

6 *Creative Kaiseki Cuisine*

6-3-9 Akasaka, Minato City

Akasaka

+81 5020180254

@shirosakaizm

Mon – Sat 5.30pm – 11pm,
Closed Sun

Reservation through its
Facebook page shirosaka.
akasaka or by phone

¥20,000

Shirosaka was recommended to me by a Japanese-British friend, whose brother works as a chef there. The food is a modern and fun take on kappo-ryori, known as kaiseki's less formal cousin, and I love this style of cuisine for its great care and beautiful preparation. The chef, Hideki Li, is Japanese, but has worked in Sydney, as well as in New York. This merging of ideas is reflected in the exciting, inventive omakase multi-course meal, with favourites such as a bowl of chutoro tuna topped with a rice cracker and filled with a quail egg and caviar, or the almost Italian pasta-like dish of noodles cooked with shrimp.

Nobu

⑦ *Sophisticated Sushi*

Nobu can hardly be described as a quintessential Japanese experience, what with the original branch opening in New York and Hollywood actor Robert De Niro being one of its founders. But it has a fun atmosphere; it's a big space so great for a lively dinner with friends (many traditional sushi restaurants are too small and quiet for groups). It also has a cool cocktail menu, with drinks such as yuzu and lychee martinis. Start with an uni shooter, followed by black cod, rock shrimp tempura and *Nobu's* signature sashimi; the desserts are divine, too. A must-visit for those wanting to try all the world's Nobus, with the added bonus of having the best sushi chefs and fish suppliers.

🏠 1F Toranomon Towers Office, 4-1-28 Toranomon, Minato City

🚇 Roppongi-Itchome

🏃 noburestaurants.com/tokyo

📷 @tokyonobu

🕐 Mon – Fri 11.30am – 1.45pm and 6pm –9.45pm,nSat 6pm –9.45pm, Sun 6pm –9.15pm

🔔 Reservation through the website or OpenTable

💲 ¥15,000

Tsutaya Roppongi

8 *Book Boutique*

I've already mentioned the *Tsutaya* book store *Daikanyama T-Site*, but the Roppongi branch is very different and well worth a visit – especially if you're staying in Roppongi or Azabu-Juban. The store has a cosy, boutique-y feel, part-bookshop, part-cafe (Starbucks), and you can sit in one of their reading nooks and browse pretty photo books while enjoying a latte and Danish pastry. It's also laptop-friendly if you need to catch up on some work and is open 21 hours a day, from 7am – 4am, so is a good spot when up early or late from jetlag.

🏠 6-1 1-1, Roppongi, Minato City

🚇 Roppongi

🏹 store.tsite.jp

📷 @tsutaya_tokyo_roppongi

⊘ Mon – Sun 7am – 4am

21_21 Design Sight

9 *Architectural Wonder*

21_21 Design Sight is a design-focused museum housed in a beautiful modern building, created by Japanese architect Tadao Ando and fashion designer Issey Miyake. Located in the garden of Tokyo Midtown in Roppongi, *21_21* is an architectural delight – worth a visit just to see the elegant concrete and glass creation itself. The lovely light space plays host to thought-provoking contemporary exhibitions throughout the year. It's a 20-minute walk from *Mori Art Museum* if you want to do an afternoon of art hopping.

⌂ 9-7-6 Akasaka, Minato City

🚉 Roppongi

↖ 2121designsight.jp

◎ #2121designsight

◷ Wed – Mon 10am – 7pm, Closed Tues

🔔 ¥1,100

Tokyo City View and Mori Art Museum

10 *Picturesque Perspectives*

For a fun two-in-one Tokyo experience, visit Mori Tower at Roppongi Hills, where you'll find the fabulous *Mori Art Museum* and the best panoramic vistas from *Tokyo City View*. The museum holds impressive exhibitions with a focus on contemporary and predominantly Asian artists. After enjoying the art, head to *Tokyo City View*, an indoor and outdoor observation deck offering stunning scenes of the city. It's especially spectacular in the evening when the city lights up. A ¥1,800 joint ticket allows access to both the art museum and the viewing deck.

🏠 53F Mori Tower, Roppongi Hills,
   Roppongi, Minato City

🚉 Roppongi

🔗 mori.art.museum, tcv.roppongihills.com

📷 @moriartmuseum, @tokyocityview

🕐 Mori Art Museum: Wed – Mon 10am – 10pm,
                   Tues 10am – 5pm
   Tokyo City View: Sun – Thurs 10am – 11pm,
                   Fri – Sat 10am –1am

💲 ¥1,800

Cote D'Azur

11 *Singing on Stage*

🏠 Rokumon 5F, 6-1-3 Roppongi, Minato City

🚇 Roppongi

🕐 Mon – Sat 12pm – 6am, Sun 12pm – 11pm

🏛 Walk-in

After dinner with Japanese friends, the automatic run of an evening will inevitably lead to a karaoke bar. This isn't about being tipsy or having a great voice, karaoke is at the heart of Japanese culture and there's no judgment or embarrassment (it's not a singing competition!). There are lots of karaoke bars around Roppongi, and our friend Yumi took us to *Cote D'Azur*, near the station. What's fun about this place is that the person singing stands on a stage complete with jazzy lights and a microphone stand. I love watching people's personalities change during karaoke, like the quiet types who come alive when belting out Bon Jovi or Madonna.

Sogetsu School of Ikebana

12 *Art of Flower Arranging*

Ikebana is the ancient Japanese art form of flower-arranging, or 'giving life to flowers'. Started by a Buddhist priest in the sixth century, ikebana went on to become an important part of Zen meditation. It was initially only allowed to be admired by 'special people', such as shogun, samurai and aristocracy (and only men!). Nowadays, everyone can enjoy ikebana and the best place to learn about it is at *Sogetsu School* in Akasaka. Foreigner-friendly, the school runs an international ikebana lesson conducted in English by welcoming and knowledgeable teachers. During the lesson, you'll learn the basic rules of ikebana, using flowers to form the three main branches, 'shin', 'soe' and 'hikae'. With classes at a reasonable ¥4,100, it's a wonderful way to spend a morning while having a true Japanese cultural experience.

Address: 7-2-21 Akasaka, Minato City

Akasaka

sogetsu.or.jp

@ikebana.sogetsu

International class every Monday 10am – 12pm

Reservation through the website

¥4,100

Harajuku

Hip Youth Hangout

The first thing that springs to mind when you mention **Harajuku** are the 'Harajuku Girls', the icons of Japanese youth fashion culture, with their fantastic outfits, make-up and accessories – a mix of overly girly pinks and edgy punk influences merged with goth, cyber and Lolita looks, a unique style and attitude that's made this small part of Tokyo a cultural centre.

These days, there are less of these cool kids parading down the streets in costume, but the celebration of this culture is still well and truly alive. Wander down lively Takeshita Street with its rows of candy-coloured shops selling Harajuku Girl-style cute clothing. Between Harajuku and Omotesando, you'll come across shopping stretches like Cat Street, filled with trendy brands and cool concept shops, as well as some great vintage stores.

Adjoining the neighbourhood is the lovely *Yoyogi Park*, a green expanse that's a welcome breath of fresh air beside the hustle and bustle of Harajuku. The large park is tranquil and serene, with the majestic *Meiji Shrine* the focal point – a peaceful place to take a pause during a busy day in the city.

HARaJUKU

to SHinjuku
↑

Meiji SHrine

10

Yoyogi PaRk
9

Harajuku

Ota Memorial
Museum of Art

FiRe St

to SHibuya
↓

HaRajuku GiRLs

⑤

Takeshita St

⑧

🚉

Meiji-jingumae
(Harajuku)

CHicago

⑦

④   ②

①   ⑥

③

to Omotesando

Good Town Doughnuts

1 *Delicious Doughnuts*

Like visiting the public baths and having a bowl of ramen, grabbing a delicious doughnut has become a daily occurrence when I'm in Tokyo. Located in the heart of Harajuku, *Good Town Doughnuts* is an American-style, Californian-inspired sweet treat shop and makes some of the best doughnuts I've tasted. I love the key lime and pistachio and they have lots of fun flavours, such as Kyoto matcha, sea salt caramel and maple bacon. If you've got a sweet tooth like me, I urge you to give these a try.

⌂ 6-12-Jingumae, Shibuya City

🚇 Meiji-jingumae (Harajuku)

↖ good-town.com

◉ @good_town_doughnuts

◷ Mon – Sun 10am – 8pm

Ⓢ ¥390

Oriental Bazaar

2 *Snazzy Souvenirs*

🏠 5-9-13 Jingumae,
Shibuya City

🚃 Meiji-jingumae
(Harajuku)

🏹 orientalbazaar.co.jp

⏱ Fri – Wed 10am – 7pm,
Closed Thurs

Oriental Bazaar was suggested to me as a good 'souvenir shop', which sounds sort of tacky, but this shop is actually quite brilliant. If you're looking for fun Japanese gifts to bring home with you, it has everything from origami-shaped chopstick rests, to shelves of sake bottles and cups, to an assortment of delicate kaiseki-style ceramics. Upstairs is a vintage and antique area with racks of secondhand kimonos, haori jackets and collectable knick-knacks. It's conveniently located on the main road between Harajuku and Omotesando, and is tax-free for foreigners (remember to bring your passport).

United Arrows

③ *Cool Clothes*

United Arrows is the most gorgeously designed shop, which you enter through a fantastic florist, with dried bouquets hanging from the ceiling and off the walls. This cool and contemporary boutique on Cat Street sells a curated collection, from high-end brands like Acne to everyday basics such as Hanes T-shirts to one-off vintage finds. It mixes and matches high and low fashion, and the space feels fun and fresh. There are a few *United Arrows* shops dotted around Tokyo; I also like the one in Shibuya and adore their sister brand *H Beauty & Youth* in Omotesando.

🏠 1F, 5-17-9 Jingumae, Shibuya City

🚃 Meiji-jingumae (Harajuku)

↖ united-arrows.co.jp

📷 @unitedarrows_official

🕐 Mon – Fri 12pm – 8pm, Sat – Sun 11am – 8pm

Opening Ceremony

④ *Cult Clothing Emporium*

In an imposing four-storey glass building on Cat Street in Harajuku, *Opening Ceremony* is a fun and fabulous shop, set up by Carol Lim and Humberto Leon, former creative directors of the fashion brand Kenzo. The store fits in with its edgy streetwear surroundings by including up-and-coming young cult designers, as well as high-fashion pieces from brands like Moschino and Vetements, alongside its own OC brand, too. The design of the store alone is worth a look, with unique features such as changing rooms in the shape of spaceships and pink-and-purple spotted and striped steps.

🏠 6-7-1-B Jingumae, Shibuya City

🚃 Meiji-jingumae (Harajuku)

📍 openingceremony.com

📷 @openingceremony

🕐 Mon – Sun 12pm – 9pm

Deus Ex Machina

Surf & Skate Store

Deus Ex Machina is a really clever, creative space combining a shop, cafe, bar and generally hip hangout in Harajuku. I really like the *Deus* concept, which is about creating community hubs in young, cool places (the sister site in Canggu, Bali, is also a fave). The stores are a physical manifestation of the lifestyles their customers aspire to lead – surfing in summer, snowboarding in winter and skating at weekends. There's a cool space in the basement that looks like a teenage boy's dream bedroom: cinema, bar, skateboards and a surfboard shaping bay beside slouchy sofas. *Deus Ex Machina* also holds twice-weekly yoga classes, on Sunday and Tuesday mornings.

🏠 3-29-5, Jingumae, Harajuku

🚇 Meiji-jingumae (Harajuku)

📍 deuscustoms.com

📷 @deusresidence

🕐 Sat – Thurs 9am – 8pm,
Fri 9am – 11pm

Champion

6 *American Basics*

There's a small but perfectly formed *Champion* clothes store on the main Cat Street strip in Harajuku, opposite *United Arrows*. Sure, this store isn't Japanese – Champion is very much an American sportswear brand – but it's my go-to shop for anything and everything basic. Pick up packs of plain-white vest tops, thick white trainer socks, cosy pastel-coloured jumpers, heavyweight T-shirts – the list goes on. Also, have a look at nearby *Champion Shibuya*, as the two stores often have different stock.

⌂ 6-14-6 Jingumae, Harajuku, Shibuya City

🚇 Meiji-jingumae (Harajuku)

↖ championusa.jp

◉ @champion_harajuku

◷ Mon – Sun 11am – 8pm

Chicago

⑦ *Japanese Thrift Shop*

Vintage stores in Tokyo can sometimes feel a tad expensive, especially considering most of their stock is imported and you can get similar items in the US and Europe. Luckily, *Chicago* is here to save the day, with four stores dotted around Harajuku, selling a mix of Western and Japanese secondhand clothing. It has a great selection of vintage kimonos, obi belts, yukatas (summer kimonos) and indigo-dyed kendogi jackets, starting from as little as ¥1,000. *Chicago* also sells cheerful American-style clothing, such as funky Hawaiian shirts and denim dungarees, as well as European tea dresses and accessories.

🏠 4-26-26 Jingumae, Harajuku, Shibuya City

🚉 Meiji-jingumae (Harajuku)

🏹 chicago.co.jp

📷 @harajukuchicago_official

🕐 Mon – Sun 11am – 8pm

Ota Memorial Museum of Art

8 *Bygone Block-Prints*

Conveniently located in Harajuku, *Ota Memorial Museum of Art* is an absolute must-visit for those interested in Japanese art and history. It showcases 'ukiyo-e' art, a traditional block-printing process popular in 17th-century Japan. The works are mostly the collection of one man, the late Seizo Ota, who amassed about 12,000 ukiyo-e pieces throughout his life. The prints exhibited change every month as the flowers, tree bark and leaves used for the pigment in ukiyo-e art fades easily. This charming and inspiring cultural collection is filled with images of Japanese mythology and fascinating stories from hundreds of years ago.

⌂ 1-10-10 Jingumae, Harajuku, Shibuya City

🚇 Meiji-jingumae (Harajuku)

🏹 ukiyoe-ota-muse.jp

◷ Tues – Sun 10.30am – 5.30pm, Closed Mon

Ⓢ ¥1,000

Yoyogi Park Flea Market

9 *Japanese Junk & Gems*

🏠 Yoyogi Park Outdoor Stage

🚃 Harajuku

📍 yoyogikoen.info

🕐 9am – 4pm
(check website for dates)

One of my favourite things to do in a new city is scout out one of the outdoor weekend flea markets. Tokyo has a few, and we were there in time for the *Yoyogi Park Flea Market* (dates can be erratic!). On a Sunday morning in February, we went searching for Japanese trinkets and treasures in the south of Yoyogi Park. Find everything from pretty plates painted with Mount Fuji, traditional Japanese dolls and decorative ceramic sake cups, to vases, rice bowls, vintage kimonos and jackets. Its location in the park means you can visit *Meiji Shrine* and Harajuku after your market visit.

Yoyogi Park and Meiji Shrine

10 *Peaceful Park*

A welcome expanse of nature in this otherwise busy and bustling city, *Yoyogi Park* is a pleasant place for a leisurely stroll and breath of fresh air. Walking through a peaceful forest, you will come across *Meiji Shrine*, a Shinto shrine dedicated to Emperor Meiji and his wife Empress Shoken. Pause to make an offering to the deities and write a wish on a small wooden tablet and hang it below a big tree. There are interesting events and festivals going on in the park throughout the year. Check out the website to see what's happening during your visit.

Yoyogi Park

Harajuku

yoyogikoen.info

Dawn to dusk

Free

Omotesando

Stylish & Sophisticated Streets

If vibrant Harajuku is for the youth, then affluent **Omotesando**, a short 10-minute stroll away, is for the grown-ups. The area is known for its high-end designer flagship stores, all vying to outdo each other with award-winning, futuristic, spaceship-style architecture. It's a great place to get in touch with Japanese creativity, from admiring beautiful buildings to discovering fashion-forward local designers.

The sophisticated area feels gentle and calm, with cosy cafes dotted around and interesting independent boutique shops among the better-known brand names. A short walk through Aoyama and you reach the hidden oasis *Nezu Museum*, a curious collection of East Asian art and home to a glorious Japanese garden with a tranquil pond.

Beyond the museum, you're in Nishi-Azabu, an upscale residential neighbourhood filled with old-school townhouses, and home to some of my favourite little restaurants in the city.

Omotesando

Aoyama - Doki Ave

to Harajuku

Omotesando

1

8

2

Aoyama Flower Market

9

11

to Shibuya

Butagumi

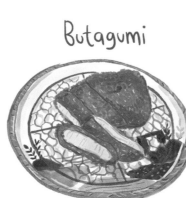

Nezu Museum

⑦

③

⑩

⑫

⑤

⑥

TORIYOSHI

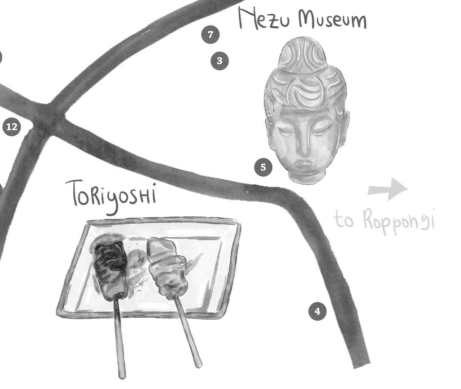

→ to Roppongi

④

Café Kitsuné

1 *Hip Coffee House*

Created by Parisian fashion label Maison Kitsuné, *Café Kitsuné* is a cool, contemporary cafe situated in a traditional, elegant wooden teahouse in the high-end enclave of Aoyama. Enter through an outdoor terrace surrounded by a bamboo-clad wall into a space decked with Japanese design details on every surface. Come for your morning coffee, or enjoy a matcha latte or green tea with delicious 'wagashi', Japanese sweets from the master makers at *Toraya*.

🏠 3-17-1 Minami Aoyama, Minato City

🚇 Omotesando

🏹 maisonkitsune.com/mk/cafe-kitsune

📷 @cafekitsune

🕐 Mon – Sun 9am – 8pm

💲 ¥560

Aoyama Flower Market

2 *Food in a Florist*

What a treat to be able to enjoy a lunch or afternoon tea in a greenhouse-style cafe surrounded by fresh flowers and foliage in the middle of Tokyo. First, you arrive at the 'flower market', a florist filled with the most stunning selection of blooms. Note: there can be a bit of a wait to get seated in the 'tea house', an enchanting space bursting with plants and flowers. For a pretty and delicious treat, try the 'Flower French toast' with seasonal fruit and edible flowers (¥1,080). Enjoy fresh blended herbal teas with lemongrass, dandelion and lemon balm.

 5-1-2 Minami Aoyama, Minato City

 Omotesando

 afm-teahouse.com

 @aoyamaflowermarket_teahouse

 Mon – Sat 11am – 9pm,
Sun 11am – 7pm

 Walk-in

$ ¥1,080

Butagumi

③ *Tasty Tonkatsu*

Located in a traditional Japanese townhouse in the residential neighbourhood of Nishi-Azabu on the edge of Omotesando, *Butagumi* can be spotted by its crescent-moon-shaped window. The restaurant has built up a strong reputation for its tonkatsu, juicy and flavoursome deep-fried breaded pork cutlets. Choose from a variety of quality pork options: 'sirloin regular', which is mildly flavoured; 'deluxe', a juicier version; 'belly', very high in fat; and 'tenderloin', the leanest cut. I went for lunch at 12.45pm and was seated quickly. Ask to sit in the nicer upstairs seating area. *Butagumi* is a six-minute walk from the *Nezu Museum*, so come before your museum visit.

🏠 2-24-9 Nishi-Azabu, Minato City

🚇 Omotesando

☎ +81 354666775

✈ butagumi.com/nishiazabu

📷 #butagumi

🕐 Tues – Sun 11.30am – 2pm and
6pm –10pm, Closed Mon

🔔 Walk-in for lunch. Reservation
required for dinner by phone

💲 ¥1,800

Toriyoshi

4 *Atmospheric Yakitori*

🏠 4-2-6 Ryowa Palace
Nishiazabu, Minato City

🚇 Roppongi or Hiroo

📷 #toriyoshi

🕐 Mon – Sun 5pm – 11pm

🔔 Walk-in

💲 ¥5,600

I really love the fun and laid-back atmosphere you get at a Japanese yakitori restaurant: no formalities and no reservations, just rows of chicken skewers grilling over hot coals. *Toriyoshi* is a bustling yakitori restaurant in the generally quiet Nishi-Azabu neighbourhood (it also has branches in Nakameguro and Ginza). We waited a while to be seated – I suggest not coming at peak hour – but eventually got a spot on the counter. We asked the chef to serve us omakase-style, for a mix of what was on the menu, and just told him to stop when we were full. This place is great value, with diner coming to ¥17,000 for three people.

97

Ushigoro S

5 *Sumptuous Barbecue*

Japanese food has been exported around the world, often very well, but Japanese barbecue – known as 'yakiniku' – is a culinary experience you'd be hard-pressed to match anywhere but on its home turf. Luckily, our friend Yumi is a yakiniku obsessive and took us to *Ushigoro S* in Nishi-Azabu where we observed Japanese skill and perfection at its finest. It's best enjoyed in a group, so book a private room and go for the 'Q' menu for the full yakiniku journey. There's a grill in the table and expert chefs will cook you dishes such as 'beef tongue with truffle' and 'Chateaubriand Mille-feuille', as well as offering raw meat like the buttery-tasting beef sashimi and beef tartare.

🏠 Barbizon 73 B1F 2-24-14, Nishi-Azabu, Minato City

🚇 Roppongi or Hiroo

☎ +81 364194129

✎ ushigoro-s.com

📷 @ushigoro_yakiniku

🕐 Mon – Sun 5pm – 12am

🔔 Reservation through the website or phone

💲 ¥14,000

Yoroniku

6 *Magnificent Meats*

Yoroniku is another fabulous Japanese barbecue 'yakiniku' restaurant in the Omotesando area. Set up in a sleek and sophisticated space, *Yoroniku* provides an impeccable experience for serious meat lovers. Order the 10-course menu and try beautiful pieces of beef prepared in as many ways, from cold beef sashimi and tartare to barbecued marinated beef shoulder, as well as rare cuts of meat. Ask in advance if you can pre-order the beef katsu sando – it will probably be the best sandwich you ever try. *Yoroniku* is a fun and lively restaurant for a group, where you can enjoy your evening huddled around a barbecue while chefs prepare tasty meat treats for your table.

🏠 Luna Rossa B1, 6-6-22 Minami Aoyama, Minato City

🚇 Omotesando

☎ +81 334984629

📷 #yoroniku

🕐 Mon – Fri 6pm – 12am, Sat 5pm – 12am, Sun 5pm –11pm

🔔 Reservation by phone

💲 ¥10,000

Taku

7 *Sublime Sushi*

Sushi is possibly Japan's most famous food export, and likely to be one of the main dishes you want to try in Tokyo. A Japanese friend suggested *Taku* when we were looking for a really great but low-key sushi restaurant – and it didn't disappoint. Located in the distinguished Nishi-Azabu neighbourhood, the small restaurant is friendly and intimate, with only eight counter seats. *Taku* feels old-school but stylish at the same time, and sushi chef Kenji Ishizaka was attentive and fun to watch. The sushi omakase is ¥21,000, which is good value considering the quantity of food, standard and setting. It's easily my top pick for a fancy sushi dinner in Tokyo.

🏠 1F, 2-11-5 Nishi-Azabu, Minato City

🚇 Omotesando

☎ +81 357744372

📷 #nishiazabutaku

🕐 Mon – Sat 6pm – 1am, Closed Sun

🔔 Reservation by phone

💲 ¥21,000

H Beauty & Youth

8 *Lifestyle Boutique*

H Beauty & Youth is a wonderfully curated, spacious boutique set over three floors. It has a cool mix of vintage and designer, as well as more affordable streetwear brands and contemporary designs. Part of the *United Arrows* umbrella company, *H Beauty & Youth* is always one of the first shops I visit when in Tokyo. In the basement is *Pizza Slice*, a playful New York-style pizza joint where – you guessed it – you can buy pizza by the slice. Why more shops don't sell delicious pizza in their basement is beyond me.

🏠 3-14-17 Minami Aoyama,
Minato City

🚇 Omotesando

↖ store.united-arrows.co.jp

📷 @h_beautyandyouth

⊘ Mon – Sun 11am – 8pm

Found Muji

9 *Curious Objects*

I've already waxed lyrical about my *Muji* obsession, so you can imagine my delight when I discovered the beautiful *Found Muji* concept store in Omotesando. Situated where the first *Muji* store opened in 1983, it's now a treasure trove of 'found' objects curated by the research team on their travels around the world and a source of inspiration for new products. Instead of the regular stationery and notebooks, find burnt-orange ceramic cups, aprons made from striped English ticking fabric, woven baskets, wooden plates and super-thin water glasses.

🏠 5-50-6 Jingumae, Shibuya City

🚇 Omotesando

📍 muji.net/foundmuji

📷 #foundmuji

🕐 Mon – Sun 11am – 9pm

Issey Miyake

10 *Japanese Innovator*

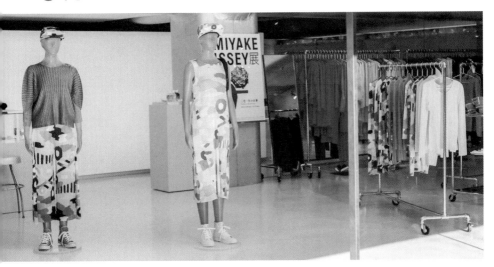

Omotesando, sponsored by *Issey Miyake*. Just joking, but it can feel like every other shop in this neighbourhood is a creative outpost of the Japanese fashion designer. With a strong and unwavering 1990s aesthetic, *Issey Miyake* is right up my street. The 'Pleats Please' shop in particular is a must-visit, selling playful and colourful clothes made with unique garment-pleating techniques, such as multicoloured jumpsuits, jazzy trousers, stripy jumper dresses, and quirky shoes and hats. Also along the road is 'Bao Bao', the brand's funky bag and accessories store.

🏠 3-17-14 Minami Aoyama, Minato City

🚇 Omotesando

📍 isseymiyake.com

📷 #isseymiyake

🕐 Mon – Sun 11am – 8pm

Farmer's Market @ UNU

11 *Weekend Market*

A lively local weekend market located between Omotesando and Shibuya, *Farmer's Market @ UNU* (United Nations University) is a wholesome place to spend your Saturday, especially when the weather's good. Find local and typical Japanese produce, such as jars of brightly coloured pickled vegetables, plus stalls of specialist tomatoes, cheeses, honey and coffee. They also have a few food trucks selling delicious curry and rice and craft cola.

🏠 5-53-70 Jingumae, Shibuya City

🚃 Omotesando or Shibuya

🔖 farmersmarkets.jp

📷 @farmersmarketjp

🕐 Sat and Sun 10am – 4pm, Closed weekdays

Nezu Museum

12 *Gorgeous Gallery*

🏠 6-5-1 Minami Aoyama,
Minato City

🚇 Omotesando

🏹 nezu-muse.or.jp

📷 #nezumuseum

🕐 Tues – Sun 10am -5pm,
Closed Mon

💲 ¥ 1,100

Nezu Museum is small but superb, showcasing a wonderful variety of exhibitions in the most stunning space. It was founded to conserve and exhibit the collection of pre-modern Japanese and East Asian art built by businessman and politician Nezu Kaichiro. Every month, the museum has a special new exhibition, showing a wide range of art mediums from painting, sculpture, calligraphy and ceramics to lacquerware and textiles. Part of its permanent collection is 'Ancient Chinese Bronzes'; view pieces such as an impeccable wine vessel that dates from 13th–11th century BC, during the Chinese Shang dynasty. Then there's the glorious garden – a quiet, perfectly formed oasis with a pretty pond and charming teahouses.

Shimokitazawa

Quirky & Quaint Quarter

Shimokitazawa is a joy of a neighbourhood. Known locally as 'Shimokita', it's a little further out from the main city centre, but only a short ride on the Metro from both Shibuya and Shinjuku Stations. It feels like its own little world and reminds me of London's Camden or New York's East Village, with its quirky little shops and dedication to vintage and secondhand clothing.

The area feels young and fun, like a less commercial Harajuku, with independent shops and restaurants catering to a creative and eclectic crowd. The streets are narrow and manageable, so you can easily wander around the whole area in a few hours during an afternoon (many shops only open after midday). With nearly every other shop selling vintage clothing, as well as a sprinkling of charming homeware stores, this is the place to go if you're looking for unique and interesting finds.

SHiMOKitaZaWa

Kamakura-DoRi Ave

5

6

Fog Linen WoRk

2

8

JaPan OPen-AiR FoLK House MuseuM

 10

9 **3**

Flamingo

4

🚌
Shimokitazawa

KaLma

7

1 HiRoKi

Hiroki

1 *Tasty Okonomiyaki*

Okonomiyaki is a comforting and delicious savoury pancake (the word 'okonomi' means 'what you like' while 'yaki' means 'grilled'). The dish often pops up on street food stalls, with different variations in every region of Japan. Located behind a tiny wooden shopfront in Shimokitazawa, *Hiroki* is a 35-year-old restaurant serving Hiroshima-style okonomiyaki, layered with noodles, vegetables and additions such as squid, shrimp and scallops. The restaurant is somewhat cosy, with space for six people seated around the main griddle, and two small two-seater tables, so it's best visited with a smaller group.

🏠 1F Honey Shimokitazawa, 2-14-14 Kitazawa, Setagaya City

🚉 Shimokitazawa

📌 teppan-hiroki.com

🕐 Mon – Sun 12 – 9.45pm

🔔 Walk-in

💲 ¥1,750

Bio Ojiyan Cafe

2 *Wholesome Cafe*

A one-minute walk from the station, *Bio Ojiyan Cafe* is a convenient choice for a healthy lunch while shopping in Shimokitazawa. It specialises in 'ojiya', a rice porridge or risotto-type dish that's both nourishing and hearty. It also offers 'teisyoku', a combination plate with varieties such as pork and ginger, which comes with rice, miso soup and little side dishes. At ¥960 a meal, it's a great-value lunch spot. It also has a branch in Harajuku.

🏠 5-35-25 Daita, Setagaya City

🚃 Shimokitazawa

📷 @bioojiyanca

🕐 Mon – Sun 11am – 9.50pm

🔔 Walk-in

💲 ¥960

Bear Pond Espresso

3 *Cult Coffee Shop*

Bear Pond Espresso has developed a cult-like status in the coffee world since it opened its doors in 2009. It was founded and run by Katsu Tanaka, who spent time living in America and says he was inspired by the 'New York taste'. His small white-fronted coffee shop is easily missed, with only a neon-pink bear-shaped sign above the door signifying his establishment. Try the classic latte and, if you're lucky, you might catch the small batch of 'Angel Stain', the signature espresso, with only 10 cups available each day.

🏠 2-36-12 Kitazawa, Setagaya City

🚌 Shimokitazawa

🡥 bear-pond.com

📷 @angelstain

🕑 Wed – Mon 11am – 5.30pm, Closed Tues

💲 ¥350

Flamingo

4 *Fabulous Used Fashion*

Shimokitazawa is all about the vintage shops, and *Flamingo* has two opposite each other in the heart of the neighbourhood. It sells mainly American pieces, handpicked by a buyer based in the US to send to Tokyo, which gives the store a tighter curation, but makes the prices higher than other vintage shops. That said, there are some really cool items of clothing here that would be hard to find anywhere else, especially its superb selection of vintage tees. There are more *Flamingo* stores in Harajuku.

🏠 Lisaville 1F, 2-25-12 Kitazawa, Setagaya City

🚉 Shimokitazawa

📷 @flamingo_shimokitazawa

🕐 Mon – Fri 12 – 9pm, Sat – Sun 11am – 9pm

Haight & Ashbury

5 *Antique Attire*

🏠 Palazina 2F, 2-37-2, Kitazawa, Setagaya City

🚃 Shimokitazawa

🏹 haightandashbury.com

📷 @haight_tokyo

⊘ Mon – Fri 1 – 9pm, Sat – Sun 12– 9pm

Haight & Ashbury is a delightful vintage store selling slightly older clothing and accessories than the other vintage shops in Shimokitazawa, most of it dating from 19th and 20th century Europe. It has a special 'antiques room' filled with delicate and high-quality original pieces, such as pearly collar attachments, beaded bags and lace dresses. It also has pieces that feel more contemporary in style, from heavy leather jackets to light white-cotton smocked shirts. Prices are on the higher end, but the quality and curation here is first-rate.

We Go

6 *Retro Wear*

I feel like I developed and fixed my fashion style as a child in the 1990s, and it hasn't moved on much since then. *We Go* is a treasure trove for nostalgia nerds like me, selling funky finds that transport you back pre-millennium. 1990s Polo Ralph Lauren is a core part of the range, from sports caps and plaid shirts to classic collared tees. *We Go* also stocks my favourite childhood pieces: 'Hard Rock Cafe' T-shirts and jumpers from Las Vegas, New York and London. It even has shelves of pink 'My Little Pony' figurines for the ultimate retro bedroom vibe.

🏠 Oak Plaza 1F, 2-29-3, Kitazawa, Setagaya City

🚇 Shimokitazawa

📍 wego.jp

📷 @wego_shimokita

🕐 Mon – Sun 11am – 9pm

Kalma

7 *Chic Vintage Boutique*

If only there were more vintage stores like *Kalma*. An antithesis to the bulging racks of clothing displayed by most secondhand shops, *Kalma* is more like a high-end boutique, offering an incredibly chic curation of original and unusual finds. Each piece is selected with love, with one-off items including a 1990s Alp sport ski jacket, bright-orange thigh-high boots, a 1940s pink beaded bag, a 1950s Western-style purple silk shirt and a pair of 1970s racing-green Champion tracksuit bottoms. Honestly, this shop feels more like a stylist's closet than a store. Items cost around ¥20-30,000.

🏠 2-16-3 Kitazawa, Setagaya City

🚇 Shimokitazawa

🏹 kalma-tokyo.com

📷 @kalma_tokyo

🕐 Mon – Fri 1– 8pm,
      Sat – Sun 1 – 7pm

Fog Linen Work

8 *Linen Lifestyle Store*

This charming shop on a side street in Shimokitazawa is the physical home of the much-loved homeware brand *Fog Linen Work*. Yumiko Sekine created the brand after trying to find the everyday linen she used as a child. She now makes her linen products in Lithuania and has a thriving wholesale business, selling in shops around the world. This store is a living manifestation of the lifestyle brand, selling gorgeous everyday items such as tea towels, napkins and tablecloths, as well as clothing and home accessories. It also has an upstairs area that is occasionally a cafe and event space.

🏠 5-35-1 Daita, Setagaya City

🚉 Shimokitazawa

🏹 foglinenwork.com

📷 @foglinenwork

⊘ Mon – Sat 12 – 6pm
Closed Sun

117

Hareginomarusho

9 *Kimono Showroom*

🏠 2-2-36-12 Kitazawa,
Setagaya City

🚉 Shimokitazawa

🏹 hareginomarusho.jp

📷 @hareginomarusho

⊘ Mon – Sun 9.30am – 6pm

Kimonos are the traditional Japanese garments worn by both men and women, particularly on special occasions such as weddings and 'coming of age days', a ceremony for 20-year-olds reaching adulthood. When I stumbled across this particular kimono shop in Shimokitazawa, what stood out were the unique and vibrant fabric designs of the ceremonial costumes. But what I really liked were the brightly coloured 'yukata' – a much lighter casual summer kimono made of cotton. Usually given to guests to wear in ryokan hotels, yukata are so comfortable – and definitely something to bring home with you.

Japan Open-Air Folk House Museum

10 *Restored Japanese Residences*

🏠 7-1-1 Masugata, Tama Ward,
Kawaski City

🚉 Mukogaoka-Yuen

🏹 nihonminkaen.jp

📷 #japanopenairfolk
housemuseum

🕐 Tues – Sun 9.30am – 5pm,
Closed Mon

💲 ¥500

Just to note, this museum isn't actually in Shimokitazawa, but it is only four stops away on the Odakyu Line. In fact, the *Japan Open-Air Folk House Museum* is a world away from the capital city, located in Kanagawa Prefecture just south of Tokyo, surrounded by thick woodland. This open-air village museum has 20 traditional 'minka' houses. Go inside a Gassho-style thatched farmhouse from early 18th-century Toyama Prefecture, with a blazing open fire, and see a 19th-century Kabuki stage used for performances from the Shima Peninsula. An interesting and interactive way to get a slice of Japan's history, the museum is uncrowded and well priced at ¥500. It also has an indigo-dyeing workshop if you're interested in local crafts.

Shinjuku

Lively & Energetic Area

Shinjuku is one of Tokyo's busiest areas, encompassing many different sides of the city depending on what you want to experience. On one side, you'll find Kabukicho; known as the seedy red-light district, it's home to many 'love hotels', as well as the narrow alleyways filled with tiny but lively bars that form *Golden Gai*.

Then you have the towering buildings with their bright neon billboard signs, behind which you'll find *Shinjuku Omoide Yokocho*, an old-fashioned lane bursting with bustling 'yakitori' eateries. Nearby, discover fabulous shopping and fashion at smart department stores and boutiques.

To counter-balance any chaos, take a relaxing stroll around the peaceful *Shinjuku Gyoen National Garden*. With its expansive grounds and interesting sites, it makes a much-needed escape from this, at times, hectic part of the city.

Isetan

Shinjuku Gyoen
National Garden

① Standing Sushi Bar

There's a huge variety of places for sushi in Tokyo, from fancy restaurants in Ginza with a six-month waiting list to low-cost walk-in-off-the-street options, such as *Standing Sushi Bar*. Diners stand around an eight-person counter and have fresh, tasty sushi served to them. For as little as ¥800 for 10 big pieces of sushi, with miso soup and tea, this is Japanese fast food at its finest.

🏠 Kasai Building 1F, 1-12-12, Nishishinjuku, Shinjuku City

🚇 Shinjuku

📷 #standingsushibar

🕐 Mon – Fri 11am-11pm, Sat-Sun 11am- 10pm

🔔 Walk-in

$ ¥800

② Mister Donut

Originally founded in the US, *Mister Donut* now only exists in Japan, with stores dotted all around the country. It sells a large assortment of different shapes and flavours, with the signature called 'pon de ring', being a light and chewy variety. The doughnuts have fun seasonal flavours, such as sakura during cherry blossom and pumpkin-shaped doughnuts during Halloween.

🏠 1-2-1 Kabukicho, Shinjuku City

🚇 Shinjuku

🏹 misterdonut.jp

📷 @misterdonut_jp

🕐 Mon – Sun 6am – 2am

$ ¥100

Shinjuku Omoide Yokocho

3 *Smoky Snacks Stands*

A fun street for an evening spent snacking on yakitori, *Shinjuku Omoide Yokocho*, which means 'memory lane', is hidden behind the bright lights of Shinjuku. Also going by the name of 'piss alley', this atmospheric and nostalgic narrow alleyway is filled with 60 or so bustling, open-fronted hole-in-the-wall restaurants, seating only a handful of customers each. Come after dark to see the red lanterns glowing and charcoal smoke billowing into the streets. A cheap and casual place to eat, expect to pay ¥2,500 each for beers and skewers.

🏠 1-2 Nishishinjuku, Shinjuku City

🚇 Shinjuku

📷 #omoideyokocho

🕐 Evening

🔔 Walk-in

💲 ¥2,500

New York Bar

4 *Scenic Drinks*

🏠 Park Hyatt Tokyo, 3-7-1-2 Nishishinjuku, Shinjuku City

🚇 Shinjuku

🏹 restaurants.tokyo.park.hyatt.co.jp/en/nyb

⊘ Sun – Wed 5pm – 12am, Thurs – Sat 5pm – 1am

🔔 Walk-in

$ ¥2,400

Having a cocktail at *New York Bar* at the Park Hyatt hotel has become an iconic Tokyo experience, made famous by the film 'Lost in Translation'. From the 52nd floor, the view over the sparkling city lit up at night is mesmerising. Get a table by the window and listen to the soft sounds of a live jazz band as you sip a martini or old-fashioned and gaze out at the Tokyo skyline. Do note that a cover charge of ¥2,500 per person applies after 8pm, or 7pm on Sundays, so it's best to come early evening.

Golden Gai

5 *Vibrant Dive Bars*

🏠 1-1-6 Kabukicho,
Shinjuku City

🚇 Shinjuku

📷 #goldengai

🕐 Evening

🔔 Walk-in

💲 ¥1,000

In the same spirit as nearby *Shinjuku Omoide Yokocho* and *Shibuya Nonbei Yokocho*, *Golden Gai* is a cluster of alleyways in Shinjuku with tiny, lively old-school bars that are fun to visit late at night. Pile into miniature bars that fit only a handful of people – you'll quickly get familiar with your neighbouring drinkers. Important to note is that many bars require a cover charge, so you might not be inclined to bar-hop as these charges will quickly rack up. Some bars are free entry, so look out for these.

Beams

6 *Creative Japanese Clothing*

Beams is an eight-storey boutique shop that sets out to celebrate all that is Japan, focusing on products with attention to craftsmanship, but in a modern, youthful and contemporary way. The Shinjuku branch is the flagship of the *Beams* retail empire, with each floor highlighting a different theme, such as 'coffee of Japan', 'clothes of Japan' and 'pop culture of Japan'. As well as *Beams*-label clothing, find collections from cult Japanese brands such as Mina Perhonen, White Mountaineering and Needles. It's a great place to pick up quality Japanese goodies for gifts to take home.

🏠 B1F - 5F, 3-32-6 Shinjuku, Shinjuku City

🚉 Shinjuku

↖ beams.co.jp

📷 @beams_japan

🕐 Mon – Sun 11am- 8pm

Isetan

7 *Delightful Department Store*

Tokyo does department stores very well, with one of the best being *Isetan* in Shinjuku. Head to the food hall on the basement level, known as the 'depachika', where you'll find all sorts of delectable nibbles, such as the classic Japanese lunch, a bento box. On the top floor is a lovely rooftop garden where you can sit and eat it. While up there, have a look at the wonderful kimono-outfitters on the seventh floor, with their swathes of sumptuous printed cloth and delicate shoes and accessories for weddings and special occasions. In the clothing section, look out for Japanese designers such as Tsumori Chisato, Marimekko and Comme des Garçons.

🏠 3-14-1 Shinjuku, Shinjuku City

🚇 Shinjuku

↗ isetan.mistore.jp

📷 @isetanparknet

🕐 Mon – Sun 10am-8pm

Thermae-Yu

8 *Sumptuous Super-Sento*

Thermae-Yu is a super-sento, a spacious serene spa located conveniently in Shinjuku. Open 24-hours a day, it's the department store of spas. It has a huge choice of spa experiences, ranging from the highly carbonated bath to the outdoor stone lying-down bath – and then there's the steam room, with vats of clay and salts to clean your skin. Using natural hot spring water transported from Nakaizu every day, Thermae-Yu is one of the most relaxing places to spend a few hours, and a quintessential Japanese bathing experience. Note: they allow foreigners with tattoos, but you'll need to cover them up.

🏠 1-1-2 Kabukicho, Shinjuku City

🚉 Shinjuku

⚲ thermae-yu.jp/hot-springs

🕑 Mon – Sun, 24-hours

$ ¥ 2,364

Shinjuku Gyoen National Garden

9 *Glorious Gardens*

🏠 11 Naitomachi, Shinjuku City

🚉 Shinjuku

🏹 env.go.jp/garden/shinjukugyoen

📷 #shinjukugyoen

🕐 9am – 4pm (Oct-Mar) – 5.30pm (Mar, June, Aug, Sept) – 6.30pm (July – Aug), Closed Mon

💲 ¥500

Shinjuku Gyoen National Garden is a sprawling park located centrally in Shinjuku. Formerly an imperial garden, it has been open to the public since 1949 and comprises a traditional Japanese garden, an English landscape garden and a French formal garden. It houses the much-photographed Kyu-Goryo-Tei or 'Taiwan Pavilion', which overlooks a pond and can be entered by visitors. Throughout the seasons, there are floral highlights such as cherry blossoms in spring (March-April), and hydrangeas and chrysanthemums in winter (Nov-Dec). Do note that opening hours change throughout the year, and the entry fee has gone up to ¥500.

Samurai Museum

10 *Medieval Armour Artifacts*

At the *Samurai Museum*, learn all about the warrior class that flourished in Japan for 700 years, from the 12th to the 19th century. Marvel at original artefacts in the armour exhibition, a display of original samurai armour, made from iron and cotton, from the Muromachi to Edo periods. The armour looks small, reflecting the 5ft average height, with elaborate helmet decorations such as moons and dragons to make the samurai warriors look taller. Upstairs, see items from the Kamakura period (1185-1333), a time when the samurai conquered Japan, and learn about the importance of the samurai sword. There are informative English guided tours that are put on every 20-25 minutes.

 2-25-6 Kabukicho, Shinjuku City

 Shinjuku

 samuraimuseum.jp

 @samuraimuseumtokyo

 Mon – Thurs 10.30am – 8.30pm, Fri-Sun 10.30am – 7.30pm

 Walk-in

 ¥1,900

Yayoi Kusama Museum

11 *Pumpkin Creations*

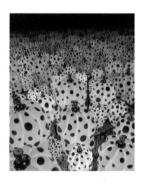

107 Bentencho,
Shinjuku City

Ushigome Yanagicho

yayoikusamamuseum.jp

#yayoikusamamuseum

Thurs – Sun 11am – 5.30pm
Closed Mon – Wed

Buy tickets in advance
through the website

¥1,000

The famous contemporary artist Yayoi Kusama must be one of Japan's most successful artist exports, with millions of visitors viewing her sell-out exhibitions all around the world. Closer to her Tokyo roots is her own museum, which opened in 2017. There are new exhibitions twice a year; I saw '*I Want You to Look at my Prospects for the Future: Plants and I*' in February 2019, a collection of oil paintings, collages and dot drawings from Kusama's childhood, during which her family owned a seed nursery business. The popular museum is small, and booking tickets in advance is essential.

Ginza & Tokyo Station

Chic District

Ginza is known for being the glitziest part of Tokyo, where well-heeled locals and tourists alike come to shop in upmarket designer boutiques and large, luxurious department stores. It's also the area most populated with high-end sushi restaurants, catering to this affluent crowd.

A 15-minute stroll from Ginza and you're in the heart of the hustle and bustle of *Tsukiji Market*. Until recently, this was the site of the city's flourishing wholesale fish market. Now, even after the move, you'll still find street food stands and small restaurants offering wonderful seafood.

A 10-minute walk north of Ginza you'll reach **Tokyo Station**, a foodie destination in itself and the gateway for exploring exciting destinations outside the city, both near and far. Do try and catch my favourite flea market, *Oedo Antique Market*, just south of Tokyo Station on the first and third Sunday of the month.

Ginza & Tokyo Station

Hoshinoya
Tokyo

1

Tokyo
Station

8

Oedo Antique Market

Ginza Corridor St

Hyatt Centric
Ginza

Ginza
Station

Muji Hotel
Ginza

6

3
5
7

Chuo-Dori

4

Kyubey

to Roppongi

2

Tsukiji Market

タラバ
50,000!

10

Sumida River

Hamarikyu
Gardens

9

Tonkatsu Suzuki

1 *Train Station Snack*

🏠 Kitchen Street, 1F,
Tokyo Station

🚉 Tokyo Station

📷 #tonkatsusuzuki

🕐 Mon – Sun 11am – 11pm

🔔 Walk-in

💲 ¥1,000

Only in Japan could you be directed to a train station to discover some seriously tasty food. You'll find *Tonkatsu Suzuki* in Kitchen Street, a cluster of casual restaurants near Yaesu North Gate in Tokyo Station. At lunchtime, expect to wait around 10 to 15 minutes for a seat, but at other times you can walk in. The counter seats give you a good view of the chefs carefully creating the breaded pork cutlets. I always have the katsu-don, a bowl of rice topped with pork cutlet and egg (¥1,000). Alternatively, have a classic pork cutlet set with cabbage and pickles.

② Tsujihan

🏠 3-1-15 Kuei Building 1F,
Nihonbashi, Chuo City

🚇 Tokyo Station

📷 #tsujihan

🕐 Mon – Sat 11am – 4pm, 5pm –9pm,
Sun 11am – 9am

🔔 Walk-in

💲 ¥1,400

Tsujihan is a 12-seater restaurant that specialises in 'kaisen-don', beautiful bowls of rice topped with fresh seafood sashimi. Halfway through your bowl, the chef adds some delicious warm dashi broth to the mix. *Tsujihan* is very popular, so avoid weekends if possible and arrive before the 11am opening time to be seated quickly.

③ Ginza Kagari Honten

Kagari is a wonderful little ramen shop specialising in 'tori paitan', which is chicken ramen – a sort of delicious Japanese chicken soup. For the reasonable sum of ¥980, you'll be given a perfectly balanced, light and smooth bowl of chicken goodness. Located down a back-alley in central Ginza, it's a great place to stop and snack while you're roaming the neighbourhood.

🏠 6-4-1-2 Ginza, Chuo City

🚇 Ginza

📷 @kagari_honten

🕐 Mon – Fri 11am – 3pm,
5.30pm – 10pm

🔔 Walk-in

💲 ¥980

Kyubey

(4) *Sushi Society*

Kyubey is a high-end sushi restaurant in Ginza and something of a Tokyo institution, having first opened its doors in 1936 under Chef Hisaji Imada. The business has been passed down through the family and is now helmed by the founder's grandson, Kagehisa Imada. Unlike the many small and intimate sushi shops, *Kyubey* is spacious and spread over five floors, making it a good option when with a group of friends. The atmosphere is lively, and the sushi chefs are friendly and knowledgeable. It's a good spot for a special sushi omakase dinner, or come earlier for the better value lunch-set.

🏠 8-7-6 Ginza, Chuo City

🚆 Ginza or Shimbashi

☎ +81 335716523

📷 #kyubeysushi

🕐 Mon – Sat 11.30am – 2pm,
5pm –10pm, Closed Sun

🔔 Reservation by phone

$ ¥20,000

Sushi Harumi

5 *Affordable Seafood*

Sushi Harumi is a well-priced sushi restaurant hidden on the fourth floor of a nondescript office building in Ginza. Top sushi restaurants in Tokyo can be incredibly expensive, so this is a good option for those without a corporate expense account. This intimate 10-seater counter restaurant offers a wonderful ¥10,000 omakase meal, serving up appetisers followed by delicious pieces of sushi placed directly on the pale wood countertop in front of you. *Sushi Harumi* is an authentic, cosy restaurant – good for those seeking somewhere between a casual sushi chain and a high-end establishment.

🏠 7-6-19, Soiree de Ginza Kiryu Building 4F, Ginza, Chuo City

🚇 Ginza

☎ +81 362285424

🔗 sushiharumi.jp

📷 #sushiharumi

🕐 Mon – Sat 5.30pm – 12am

🔔 Reservation through Pocket Concierge or by phone

💲 ¥10,000

Little Smith

6 *Discreet Drinking Den*

🏠 KN Building B2F, 6-4-12
Ginza, Chuo City

🚌 Ginza

☎ +81 355681993

🏹 littlesmith.net

🕐 Mon – Fri 6pm – 3am,
Sat 6pm – 1am, Closed Sun

🔔 Walk-in or reserve by phone

💲 ¥2,000

Although I wouldn't class myself as a barfly, I do appreciate a really well-made cocktail once in a while, so I was delighted to stumble across *Little Smith* after dinner in Ginza. Located in a dimly lit basement, it has a hefty oval-shaped polished-walnut bar and smart mixologists in white suits and black bow ties creating cocktails in any flavour you fancy. The yuzu martini is great, as are the fresh strawberry and cucumber concoctions. Do note that, like many bars, it has a cover charge of ¥1,500 per person.

Dover Street Market

(7) *Fashion Front-Runner*

The eclectic clothing store *Dover Street Market* first launched in London, but its Tokyo outpost in Ginza is DSM's star attraction. Find seven floors of fabulous fashion, with each level featuring a range of artworks and inspiring installations as well as clothes. Founded by Rei Kawakubo of Comme des Garçons and her husband, the store stocks her brand and other high-end labels such as Gucci, Rick Owens, Simone Rocha and Japanese label Undercover, as well as collaborations with Nike. The design of the store is a marvel in itself, so it's worth a visit even if you don't plan to buy anything.

🏠 Ginza Komatsu West 6-9-5, Ginza, Chuo City

🚇 Ginza

📍 ginza.doverstreetmarket.com

📷 @doverstreetmarketginza

🕐 Mon – Sun 11am – 8pm

Oedo Antique Market

8 *Remarkable Relics*

Oedo Antique Market is a marvellous large outdoor fair held on the first and third Sunday of each month, conveniently located near Tokyo Station. There isn't a huge amount of antique or vintage homeware shops in Tokyo, so if you're looking for old, interesting and unique Japanese items for your home, then this is the place. Browse from a choice of 250 stallholders selling everything from red-painted kokeshi dolls, antique masks, vintage ceramics and all sorts of curiosities and trinkets collected by local sellers. Be sure to stop by the Japanese print stall, selling original brightly coloured ukiyo-e woodblock prints that are hundreds of years old.

⌂ Tokyo International Forum, 3-5-1 Marunouchi, Chiyoda City

🚇 Tokyo Station or Yurakucho

🔗 antique-market.jp

📷 #oedoantiquemarket

🕐 1st and 3rd Sunday of the month, 9am – 4pm

Hamarikyu Gardens

9 *Picturesque Park*

This gorgeous Japanese landscaped garden is an oasis of tranquility just a short walk from bustling Ginza and *Tsukiji Market. Hamarikyu Gardens* is joyfully uncrowded and is beautifully designed, with bridges, ponds and teahouses dotted around. During each season there are different flowers to enjoy. I visited the garden in March and saw fields of bright-yellow rapeseed flowers and pretty pink plum trees in bloom. After wandering around the gardens, have a traditional tea experience at *Nakajima Tea House*, where they serve green tea and wagashi sweets with views over the gardens.

🏠 1-1 Hamarikyuteien, Chuo City

🚇 Shiodome

📷 #hamarikyugardens

🕐 Mon – Sun 9am – 4.30pm

💲 ¥300

Tsukiji Market

10 *Bustling Bazaar*

You might have heard that the wholesale fish market at *Tsukiji*, famous for its tuna auctions, has moved to a new site in *Toyosu Market*. But, despite this move, *Tsukiji's* 'Outer Market' remains open and is doing as brisk a business as ever. There's a vibrant atmosphere at *Tsukiji Market*, a cluster of narrow alleyways with low-rise buildings filled with hundreds of tiny food stalls. You can sample various types of seafood here, from sushi and uni, to crab and unagi. It's also a great place to pick up Japanese kitchen items and ceramics. Arrive early before the crowds descend, and spend a few hours trying the variety of snacks on offer.

🏠 5-2-1 Tsukiji, Chuo City

🚇 Tsukiji

➹ tsukiji.or.jp

📷 #tsukiji

⊘ Morning

Ueno & Ryogoku

Cultural Communities

Located northeast of the centre of Tokyo, **Ueno** is a cultural hub with a cluster of museums, including Japan's oldest and largest, *Tokyo National Museum* – an enlightening must-visit institution situated in picturesque Ueno Park. During spring, the park is a popular spot for 'hanami', the Japanese custom of cherry-blossom viewing.

Below Ueno and east over the Sumida River is **Ryogoku**, the historical heartland of sumo wrestling – the ultimate sporting activity representing Japanese traditions and customs. With the stadium *Ryogoku Kokugikan* at the centre of activities, the area revolves around the sumo wrestling industry, from the sumo stables where wrestlers train, to the restaurants serving 'chankonabe', a high-calorie stew to aid weight gain. Don't miss a visit to the exciting sumo-wrestling tournaments held at the stadium in January, May and September of each year.

UENO & RYOGOKU

Tokyo National Museum

4

2

Inshotei

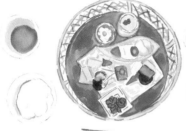

1

Ueno Park

Ueno

Ueno Line

Kanda River

Ohya Shobo

6

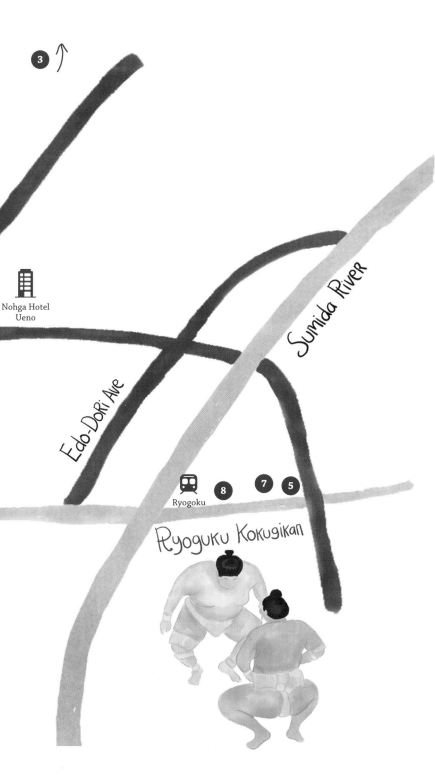

3 ↑

Nohga Hotel
Ueno

Sumida River

Edo-Dori Ave

Ryogoku 8 7 5

Ryoguku Kokugikan

Inshotei

1 *Delicate Dishes*

Inshotei is an enchanting restaurant, located in what looks like a rambling, ramshackle old wooden house in the middle of leafy Ueno Park. Established in 1875 as a manor house for overseas guests, the building is now a traditional kaiseki-style eatery, where every diner is able to enjoy gorgeous views of the park from vast glass windows. They do wonderful lunch sets, beautifully presented and almost too pretty to eat. I had the 'Hanakagozen Tuki' set (¥2,600), with grilled fish, 15 different seasonal vegetables, sides of miso and chawanmushi and a small dessert of mocha wrapped in a green leaf. After lunch, head to the *Tokyo National Museum*, a 10-minute walk from *Inshotei*.

🏠 4-59 Ueno Park, Taito City

🚇 Ueno

☎ +81 338218126

🏹 innsyoutei.jp

📷 @inshotei

🕐 Mon – Sun 11am – 3pm,
5pm – 11pm

🔔 Reservation through the
website

💲 ¥2,600

Tokyo National Museum

2 *Enthralling Objects*

Founded in 1872, *Tokyo National Museum* displays a captivating collection of Asian art and antiques in a cluster of large buildings in Ueno Park. I particularly enjoyed the main Honkan building, housing Japanese artworks including prehistoric clay figurines or 'dogu' of the Jomon period (1000-300 BC) and folding screen and door paintings from the more recent Edo period. Walk through rooms displaying the Noh masks and costumes of the Uesugi clan, once used by the warrior class in masked-drama performances in the Edo period. And learn about the daily lives of the Ainu people from the north and the Ryukyuan people from the south of Japan, each with their unique cultures.

🏠 13-9 Ueno Park, Taito City

🚇 Ueno

↖ tnm.jp

📷 @tokyonationalmuseum

🕐 Tues, Wed, Thurs, Sun 9.30am – 4.30pm, Fri – Sat 9.30am – 9pm, Closed Mon

💲 ¥620

Maenohara Onsen Sayano Yudokoro

3 *Open-Air Bathing*

As you can tell from a brief flip through this book, visiting an onsen is one of my favourite activities to do in Japan. My top pick in Tokyo has to be the marvellous *Maenohara Onsen Sayano Yudokoro*, located to the north of the city near Shimurasakaue Station. The main appeal is the 'rotenburo' outdoor bathing area, designed to give you the feeling of being deep in the Japanese countryside. Sit beneath the sky in a pot-shaped bath or in a relaxing lie-down bath. The onsen is slightly out of the city centre, a 35-minute journey on the Mita Line from Otemachi Station, but it's worth the trip as you could easily spend all day at these heavenly hot springs.

🏠 3-41-1 Maenocho, Itabashi City

🚇 Shimurasakaue

↖ sayanoyudokoro.co.jp

📷 @sayanoyudokoro

🕐 10am – 1am

💲 ¥870

④ Haginoyu

🏠 2-13-13 Negishi, Taito City

🚇 Uguisudani

🏹 haginoyu.jp

🕐 Mon – Sun 6am – 9am, 11am – 1am

$ ¥530

After a few hours spent wandering around *Tokyo National Museum*, you're going to want to recoup. Head to the swish and modern sento *Haginoyu*, a 15-minute walk from the museum. Opened in 2017, this contemporary public bath is splendidly spacious and offers an assortment of bathing experiences. Note: they have a no-tattoos policy.

⑤ Edoyu

A large, clean and modern sento in Ryogoku, *Edoyu* is slightly more expensive than other public baths, but the variety of options here means you can spend a few hours having a proper spa experience. Hop between the super-jet bath, the Chinese herbal-medicine bath and the relaxing bedrock baths.

🏠 1-5-8 Kamezawa, Sumida City

🚇 Ryogoku

🏹 edoyu.com/ryougoku

🕐 Mon – Sun 11am – 9am

$ ¥2,700

Ohya Shobo

6 *Publications of the Past*

As someone who creates books, I was delighted to come across *Ohya Shobo* in Jimbocho, a fascinating antique bookstore with all the charm of Harry Potter's 'Flourish and Blotts'. This small shop sells beautiful editions from the Edo period (1603-1868), when 'Kusazochi' woodblock-printed illustrated books were a prominent part of the city's culture. Step back in time and immerse yourself in illustrated storybooks, poetry and literature, decorated with exquisite woodblock designs. The shop also sells ukiyo-e woodblock prints by famous artists, as well as old travel maps.

🏠 1-1 Kanda Jimbocho, Chiyoda City

🚇 Jimbocho

⚑ ohya-shobo.com

🕐 Mon – Sat 10am – 6pm, Closed Sun

Edo-Tokyo Museum

(7) *History of Tokyo*

Edo-Tokyo Museum is handily located next door to the sumo stadium *Ryogoku Kokugikan* and is a great way to spend a couple of hours before the wrestling starts. The museum gives visitors a glimpse of life in 'Edo', the former name for Tokyo, over the last 400 years. See miniature replica towns, moats and roads from the 17th century and look at life-size models of houses where regular people lived called 'munewari nagaya', buildings divided to create several residences. Learn about the unique publishing culture of Edo, with its early manga culture and 'kibyoshi' woodblock-printed comic books.

🏠 1-4-1 Yokoami, Sumida City

🚉 Ryogoku

📍 edo-tokyo-museum.or.jp

📷 @edotokyomuseum

🕐 Tues – Fri, Sun 9.30am – 5.30pm,
Sat 9.30am – 7.30pm,
Closed Mon

💲 ¥600

Sumo Wrestling – Ryogoku Kokugikan

8 *Sumo Stadium*

Sumo wrestling is Japan's national sport and ultimate spectator activity. The Grand Sumo Tournaments are held over two weeks in January, May and September at the *Ryogoku Kokugikan* venue in east Tokyo. More than just a sporting event, sumo is an intrinsic part of Japanese culture, tracing its origins back 1,500 years, with ancient traditions and ceremonies still performed today. Referees look more like priests, wrapped in luxuriously thick brightly coloured silk robes and black hats. Doors open at 8am, with preliminary bouts in the morning and the more exciting bouts later in the day. I entered at 2.30pm for the 2.40pm Juryo bouts. The top wrestlers come on at 5.30pm for the final bouts and, afterwards, the wrestlers perform the centuries-old bow-twirling ceremony called 'Yumitori-shiki'.

🏠 1-3-28 Yokoami, Sumida City

🚇 Ryogoku

✦ sumo.or.jp

📷 #ryogokukokugikan

🕗 8am – 6pm during tournament days

🔔 See 'Getting tickets'

Getting tickets

In advance
- Advance tickets are released about a month before the tournament, e.g. in August for a September tournament.
- Tickets can be purchased online at sumo.pia.jp/en
- There are two types of tickets:
    1. Japanese box seating for four people: from ¥38,000
    2. Arena seats: from ¥3,800
- You can also buy tickets from resellers such as viator.com or govoyagin.com (although these will be more expensive).

On the day
- 400 on-the-day 'free seat' tickets are available to buy on the door at *Ryogoku Kokugikan*. Queue up at the stadium no later than 7.20am, in time for the ticket office opening at 7.45am. You will be given a numbered queue ticket, after which you can proceed to buy your ticket, which costs ¥2,200. Note, these are the cheap seats, but many seats in the stadium are often empty, so you could sit further forward until someone comes to claim them.

Near Tokyo

Mountainous Regions

I always think how wonderful it would be to live in Tokyo – not just to be in the vibrant city itself, but to be able to access the assortment of amazing areas that are only an hour or two away. My favourite area nearby is **Hakuba**, a cosy ski resort located in the magnificent Japanese Alps in Nagano Prefecture. The mountains are uncrowded, and it's a joy to sample sushi after an active day on the slopes.

Between Hakuba and Tokyo is the resort town of **Karuizawa**, a laid-back highland region that's especially appealing when the temperatures in Tokyo climb too high.

Southwest of Tokyo is the delightful hot-springs town **Hakone**, a convenient and pleasant escape – particularly during the cold winter months. Not far from Hakone is the majestic **Mount Fuji**, an icon of Japan and an enjoyable destination for outdoor activities.

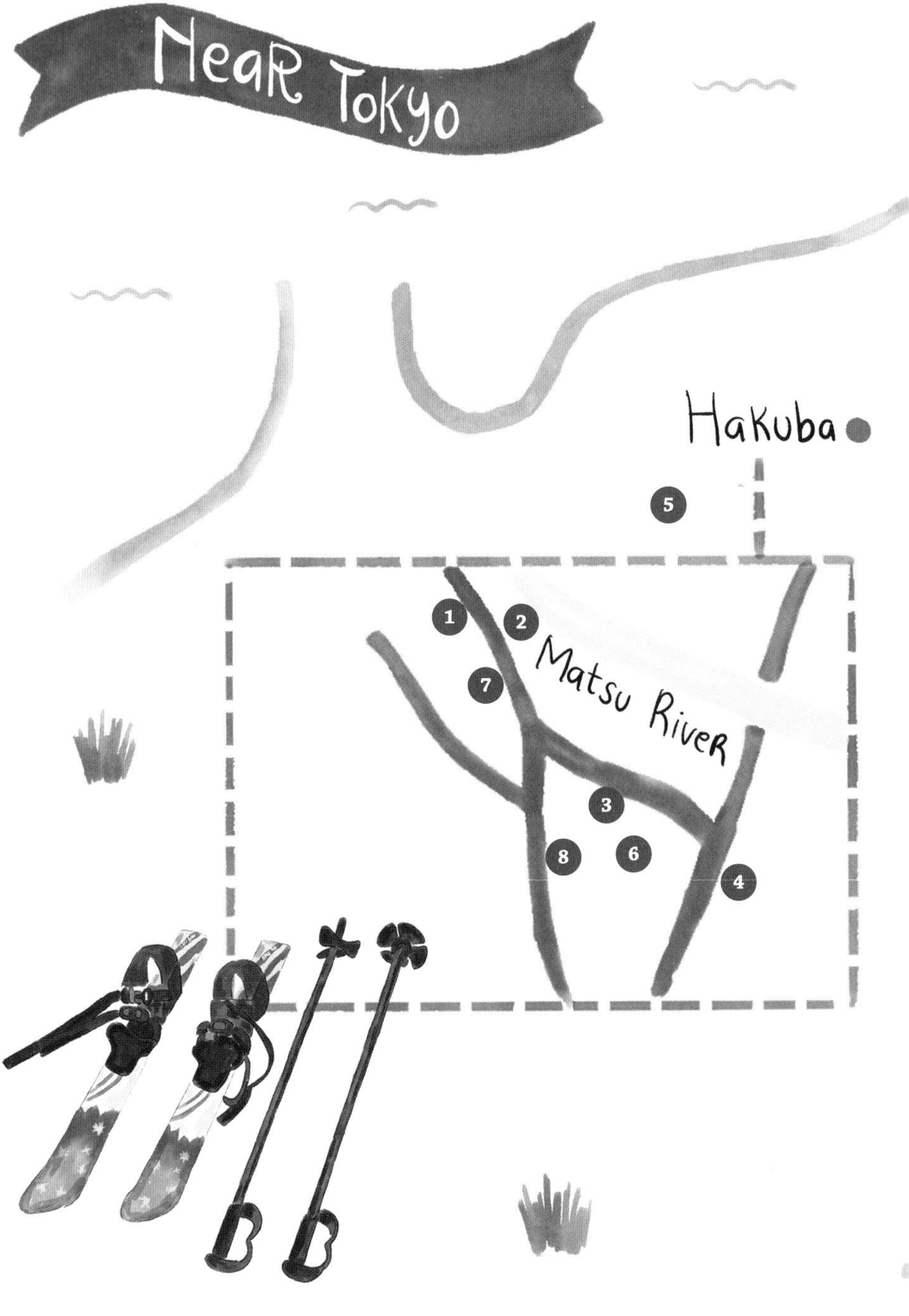

Near Tokyo

Hakuba

Matsu River

Hakuba

250km northwest of Tokyo lie the majestic Japanese Alps in Nagano Prefecture, conveniently accessed by train from Tokyo Station. **Hakuba** is a charming ski resort near Nagano, (Nagano is best known for hosting the 1998 Winter Olympics); the perfect place for a fun few days of snow sports. The mountain range is stunning and worth visiting for the views alone. While out and about on the slopes, enjoy katsu curry and karaage chicken for lunch. After a hard day's skiing, have a hot soak in an outdoor onsen overlooking the snowy mountains. Come evening enjoy a delicious local Japanese dinner while warming up on hot sake.

Getting there

- From Tokyo Station take the Hokuriku-Shinkansen line to Nagano Station. The journey takes 1hr 32 mins and costs ¥8,000 (or use a JR Pass).
- From Nagano Station take the bus to Hakuba bus terminal. This takes around 1hr 15 mins and costs ¥1,800.

Mountain Side

1 *Slope-side Abode*

Mountain Side is a modern ski-in ski-out apartment block with arguably the best location in Hakuba, being a stone's throw from Happo Kokusai ski lift. Enjoy a stunning panoramic view of the mountain range through floor-to-ceiling windows. With a group of friends, we stayed in a three-bedroom apartment, which had a large, cosy lounge area and a good-sized kitchen. *Mountain Side* has a helpful concierge and a very useful shuttle bus service to drop you at lifts, the supermarket and restaurants.

 4314-1 Kitashiro, Kitaazumi-gun, Hakuba

 Hakuba

 mountainsidehakuba.com

 @mountainsidehakuba

$ From ¥65,000 per night for 3-bed apartment in winter

Phoenix Cocoon

2 *Cosy Chalet*

🏠 4982-2 Hokujo,
Kitaazumi-gun, Hakuba

🚉 Hakuba

🏹 phoenixhotel.jp/phoenix-chalets/phoenix-cocoon/

💲 From ¥100,000 per night for 3-bed apartment in winter

For a more chalet-like feel, *Phoenix Cocoon* is a contemporary cabin nestled in Wadano Forest near Happo Village. With underfloor heating and big comfy sofas in the living area, this chalet is super-cosy and comfortable. Arranged over two floors, it feels both spacious and private. We stayed with friends in a three-bedroom chalet with a large kitchen equipped for home-cooked dinners. *Phoenix Cocoon* has a car you can use, but remember to bring an international driving licence.

3 Zen

🏠 3020-49 Hokujo, Hakuba

🕐 Thurs, Fri, Sun and Mon 11am – 2pm and 5.30 – 8pm, Sat 5.30pm – 8.30pm, Closed Tues and Wed

🔔 Walk-in

$ ¥1,500

Located in Hakuba village, *Zen* is a great place for an authentic lunch of handmade soba noodles. Set in a traditional Japanese house, the restaurant has tatami-floor seating as well as Western-style seated tables. Order the 'Tenzaru' set with cold soba and a plate of seafood and vegetable tempura for ¥1,500.

4 Kikyo-ya

🏠 1909-1 Hakubacho, Hakuba

☎ +81 261723633

🕐 Wed – Mon 11.30am – 2pm and 5.30pm – 10pm, Closed Tues

🔔 Walk-in or reservation by phone

$ ¥3,350

A fantastic spot for some post-ski sushi, *Kikyo-ya* is a quaint, old-fashioned restaurant where you sit on the floor and are served up divine dishes of fresh seafood. Order 10 pieces of the freshest sushi for ¥3,350.

5 Kitaguni Lodge

🏠 Hakuba Cortina

🔔 Walk-in

$ ¥2,000

A slope-side canteen located in the nearby ski resort of Hakuba Cortina, *Kitaguni Lodge* is fairly basic, but has a nostalgic charm with chintzy floral tablecloths and net curtains on the windows. It has great views of the mountains and does a mean katsu curry – and the karaage is good too.

6 Wagyu Kobeya

🏠 2443-1 Misorano, Hakuba

☎ +81 261725382

🏹 windy-kobeya.com

🔔 Reservation by phone

💲 ¥5,000

Wagyu Kobeya is a fun restaurant for meat-lovers – as the name suggests, it's known for its premium Wagyu beef, and Kobe beef in particular. Yakiniku-style (Japanese barbecue), you sit around tables with an in-built grill and cook the pieces of meat and veg yourself.

7 Yamagami Syokudou NEO

🏠 4086 Hokujo, Hakuba

🔔 Walk-in

💲 ¥2,200

Yamagami is a casual and lively spot for good gyoza, located in the heart of Hakuba village. You may need to wait a while to get a seat, but once in you can order the party plate of gyoza, with 30 dumplings for a very reasonable ¥2,200.

8 B.O.S

🏠 3020-1100, Hokujo, Hakuba

☎ +81 261850362

🔔 Reservation by phone

💲 ¥3,000

A shoebox of a restaurant, *B.O.S* is a quirky one-man-band set-up, serving up generous portions of delicious okonomiyaki (Japanese savoury pancakes). It has typical traditional tatami-floor seating and low-rise tables, which can be a squeeze! Ask your hotel or chalet to make a booking for you in advance.

Karuizawa

Karuizawa is a chic resort town at the foot of Mount Asama in Nagano Prefecture. 150km north of Tokyo, and just over an hour by train, the town is a favourite among local artists, writers and celebrities looking for a cool highland retreat to escape to during the hot Tokyo summers. Loved by everyone from John Lennon and Yoko Ono to the Imperial family, Karuizawa is a calm and serene region known for its beautiful scenery, abundant nature and outdoor lifestyle. I visited in the height of summer, when the humidity of Tokyo got too much. I loved the cool, fresh air and tranquil atmosphere that envelops the region.

Getting there

- Karuizawa is really quick and easy to get to from Tokyo. Go to Tokyo Station and take the Hokuriku-Shinkansen (JR) to Karuizawa Station.
- The journey takes about 1h 18 mins and costs ¥5,910.

Hoshinoya Karuizawa

9 *Mountain Resort*

In early September, we left a hot 32°C (89°F) day in Tokyo for a fresh 23°C (73°F) in elevated Karuizawa. *Hoshinoya Karuizawa* is a secluded village-like resort inspired by the nature that surrounds it. Rooms are designed to feel like modern forest cabins, with balconies overlooking a small lake with wide-reaching views over woodlands. Relaxing activities include enjoying a 'meditation bath' and for nature-lovers, there is on-site wildlife research centre Picchio, where you can watch musasabi (Japanese flying squirrels) at night. The dining room is tiered like rice field terraces and dinner is traditional kaiseki cuisine, prepared using local seasonal produce from the mountain region.

🏠 2148 Nagakura, Karuizawa

🚆 Karuizawa Station

⬧ hoshinoya.com/karuizawa

📷 @hoshinoya.official

💲 From ¥51,600

Hakone

Hakone is an enchanting mountainous region 85km southwest of Tokyo. The train journey to get there is in itself charming; Hakone Tozan Railway is Japan's oldest mountain railway, weaving through bamboo and pine trees, and over bridges suspended over valleys. Famous for its hot springs, for hundreds of years Hakone has been a favourite onsen destination for Tokyoites looking to escape the city.

Getting there

- Take the train from Shinjuku Station to Hakone-Yumoto Station.
- The journey takes 1h 34 mins on the Romancecar and costs ¥2,280.

Hakone Kamon

10 *Real Ryokan*

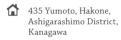
435 Yumoto, Hakone, Ashigarashimo District, Kanagawa

Hakone-Yumoto

hakone-kamon.jp

#hakonekamon

¥57,000

Hakone is filled with fantastic hot-spring ryokan hotels. A ryokan is a traditional Japanese inn with tatami-matted rooms, a public bath and exquisite service – a must-do experience when visiting Japan. With a Japanese friend, we stayed a night at *Hakone Kamon*, an authentic ryokan with modern additions such as Western beds and local touches such as a private onsen on the balcony. The ryokan has an amazing public bath area with the feel of an old country-village, offering 10 different types of bathing experiences and is especially atmospheric at night. It also does a wonderful kaiseki dinner, which you sit down and eat wearing a yukata that they provide. Hot-spring ryokans can be expensive, but this one also offers a 'day plan' where you can come for lunch and use the hot-spring baths for ¥2,500.

173

Hakone Open-Air Museum

11 *Splendid Sculptures*

If you make the trip to Hakone, don't leave without visiting the wonderful *Hakone Open-Air Museum*. Set against the backdrop of the rolling hills of Fuji-Hakone-Izu National Park, the museum has an astonishing collection of sculptures by the world's most celebrated artists. Encounter the towering figure of 'Balzac' by French sculptor Auguste Rodin and marvel at 'Reclining Figure' by British artist Henry Moore. Within the museum is an extraordinary Picasso collection featuring 319 pieces of his work, centred around ceramics and his brilliant ink paintings of bullfighting. You can also see sculptures from Japanese artists such as Taro Okamoto and Yasuo Mizui.

🏠 1121 Ninotaira, Hakone, Ashigarashimo District, Kanagawa

🚇 Chokoku-no-Mori

⚲ hakone-oam.or.jp

📷 #hakoneopenairmuseum

⊘ Mon – Sun 9am – 5pm

💲 ¥1,600

Owakudani

12 *Volcanic Valley*

Owakudani, known as the 'Great Boiling Valley', is a volcanic zone around a crater created during the last eruption of Mount Hakone, 3,000 years ago, and there's still high volcanic activity today. *Owakudani* is reached by taking the Hakone Ropeway, a cable car from Sounzan Station, after riding on the funicular Hakone Tozan Cable Car. Your experience is decided by the weather. On a clear day, there are far-reaching views to Mount Fuji and the smoky sulphuric valley. On a cloudy day, you might only get to enjoy the 'kuro-tamago' – eggs that turn black after being boiled in the sulphurous water – which are sold at the site.

🏠 Sengokuhara, Hakone, Ashigarashimo District, Kanagawa

🚇 Owakudani

📍 hakoneropeway.co.jp

📷 #owakudani

🕐 Mon – Sun 9am – 5pm

💲 ¥840

Mount Fuji

Mount Fuji is the symbol of Japan. For centuries, the sacred snow-capped volcano has been the object of worship and pilgrimage and has inspired countless paintings and poems. Today, both locals and visitors to Japan enthusiastically admire 'Fujisan', Japan's highest mountain, standing at 3,776m tall. Mount Fuji is situated 100km southwest of Tokyo and can be reached in about two hours. You can enjoy outdoor activities in the surrounding lakes and, during the summer climbing season from July to mid-September, it is possible to hike to the summit.

Getting there

- An easy way to get to from Tokyo to Mount Fuji is by bus. Go to the bus terminal at Shinjuku Station and get a bus to Kawaguchiko Station.
- The journey takes about 1hr 50 mins and costs ¥1,950.

Hoshinoya Fuji

13 *Scenic Retreat*

🏠 1408 Oishi,
Fujikawaguchiko

🚃 Kawaguchiko Station

🏹 hoshinoya.com/fuji

📷 @hoshinoya.official

💲 From ¥43,800

The word 'glamping', used to describe 'glamorous camping', definitely applies here. While there are no tents at *Hoshinoya Fuji*, the small resort cheerfully celebrates the outdoors and all it has to offer. The cabins are designed minimally but are comfortable and cosy, with a focus on the majestic views of Mount Fuji. There are super communal areas such as the 'cloud terrace', wooden platforms that seemingly float in the woods, with campfires and cosy hammocks in the trees. Have dinner outside in the forest kitchen, where you'll sit under a warm 'kotatsu' (a hot table). In the morning, head for an early canoe on Lake Kawaguchi and hope that Fujisan isn't hiding behind the clouds!

Kyoto & Around

History & Heritage

Kyoto is regarded as the cultural centre of Japan, a city and region steeped in rich history and heritage. It lies 480km west of Tokyo, which in most countries would feel far, but that's a mere two hours on Japan's high-speed bullet train. Compared to Tokyo's modern structures, Kyoto's widespread 'machiya' – traditional wooden houses – look altogether ancient. Despite fires and earthquakes, the temples and sights in and around Kyoto are in meticulous condition and a wonder to witness.

South of Kyoto is the equally cultural city of **Nara**. The capital of Japan in the 8th century, Nara is now well known for the deer that roam its old temples.

Venture south into Wakayama Prefecture to the Shingon Buddhist town of **Mount Koya**, or 'Koyasan', part of a pilgrimage route for centuries. Experience sleeping in a 'shukubo' – Buddhist temple lodging – and join in with Morning Prayer.

Kyoto & Around

Todai-ji Temple

Osaka ●
19
20
22 23
Nara
18 21

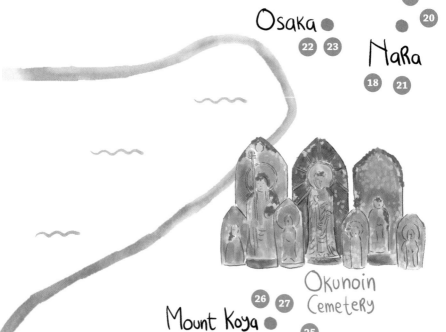

Okunoin
Cemetery
26 27
Mount Koya ●
24 25

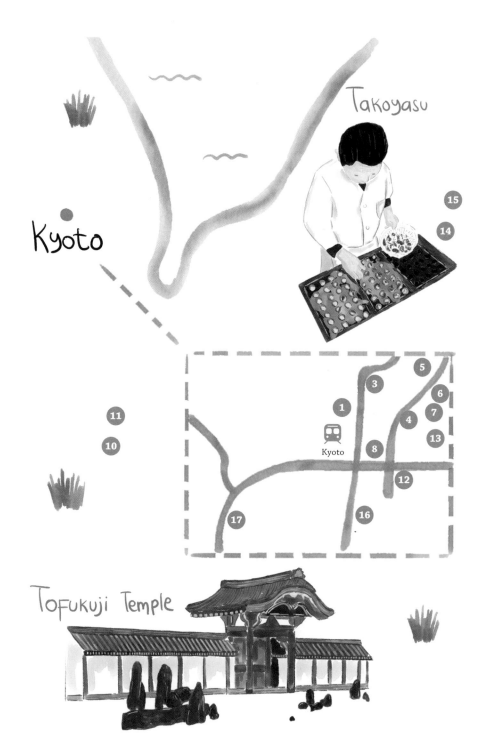

Kyoto

For over a thousand years, from 794 to 1868, **Kyoto** was the capital of Japan and is still regarded as the cultural center of the country. Home to hundreds of beautiful Buddhist temples, Shinto shrines, tranquil gardens and palaces, it has been historically preserved, having luckily avoided the damages that hit other parts of Japan (including Tokyo) in WWII. Located in the Kansai region in southern-central Japan, Kyoto is surrounded by three mountains – Higashiyama, Kitayama and Nishiyama.

Getting to and around Kyoto

From Tokyo
From Tokyo Station take the Tokaido-Sanyo Shinkansen train to Kyoto Station. This takes around 2hrs 18 mins and trains are frequent. A one-way ticket costs ¥13,910 or you can use a JR pass.

Travelling around Kyoto
The easiest way to get around Kyoto is of course by taxi, which is especially helpful with a packed itinerary as places can be quite far from each other. Buses are an easy and affordable alternative (Google Maps has the bus routes). Cycling is a fun way to get around – there are bike rental stores throughout the city. Walking is fine during the cooler months.

Malda Kyoto

① *Artisanal Accommodation*

A façade of latticed sugi cedarwood sets a modern, minimal tone for *Malda Kyoto*. The brainchild of Tokyo architect Nobuyuki Fujimoto, the hotel has just three guestrooms, each on a separate level and themed around a single Japanese colour: 'aka' (red), 'ao' (blue) and 'sumi' (charcoal grey). All are spaciously stylish, with bold textiles and stone floors. The hotel was inspired by the philosophies of Jurgen Lehl, the late Japan-based German designer renowned for his passion for sustainability. Luckily for guests, his products – and many items in the hotel, from textiles to teacups – can be found in the *Babaghuri Kyoto* store just opposite.

🏠 604-8106 Kyoto, Nagagyou City

🚉 Kyoto Shiyakusho-mae

🏹 maldakyoto.com

📷 @malda.kyoto

💲 From ¥48,000

② Ryokan Ryokufuso

Ryokan Ryokufuso is an affordable and foreigner-friendly traditional Japanese 'ryokan' hotel. Rooms are authentically minimal, with tatami flooring, low-slung tables and chairs, and Japanese futon bedding, which is put out for you at night and stored in a cupboard during the day. Further customary elements include a yukata to wear and a pot of natural green tea to make in your room. On the sixth floor there's a relaxing public bath, with views over the rooftops of Kyoto, which is open in the evenings and mornings.

🏠 600-8323 Kyoto, Shimogyo City

🚇 Gojo

🏹 ryokufuso.jp

📷 @kyoto_ryokan_ryokufuso

$ From ¥15,000

③ Airbnb

Kyoto has an abundance of quirky and unique homes to stay in, many of which can be booked on Airbnb. Stay in a 'machiya', a traditional wooden townhouse often with tatami flooring and lovely small Zen gardens. Some are old and authentic where as others have had modern renovations.

🏹 airbnb.com

4 Mendokoro Kato

On my first visit to Kyoto, we stumbled across this quaint soba restaurant while wandering around the Gion district. *Mendokoro Kato* serves delicious handmade soba, which you can see being prepared in the tiny home-style kitchen. There's no listing on Google, so search for 'Pooh's cafe' and you'll find it opposite. Go for lunch and get a generous side of tempura with your cold soba with dipping sauce.

🏠 605-0066 Higashiyama-dori Ave (opposite Pooh's cafe)

🚃 Higashiyama

🕐 Daytime

🔔 Walk-in

💲 ¥2,000

5 Takoyasu

This fun street food stand serves tasty 'takoyaki' – a Japanese snack of octopus balls fried in batter and topped with brown sauce and bonito flakes. Although this dish originates in nearby Osaka, I much prefer the takoyaki I tried at *Takoyasu* as they use really big chunks of octopus. And it's far enough away from the tourist areas that they have to make it really good! Come in the evening for a quick pre-dinner snack.

🏠 57-3 Okazaki Iriecho, Sakyo Ward

🚃 Higashiyama

🕐 Mon – Sun 4pm – 1.30am

🔔 Walk-in

💲 ¥600 for 8 pieces

⑥ Okakita

Okakita is a calm and minimal space serving tasty, warming bowls of udon and soba. Located in a picturesque 'machiya', townhouse, the restaurant has a serene Zen garden in the back. Order cold soba with delicious dipping sauce, or a big hearty bowl of udon, which comes with tempura.

🏠 34 Okazaki Minamigoshocho, Sakyo Ward

🚇 Higashiyama

🕐 Thurs – Mon 11am – 6pm, Closed Tues – Wed

🔔 Walk-in

💲 ¥1,200

⑦ Yamamoto Menzou

Next door to Okakita is the very popular Yamamoto Menzou, a dark and dingy no-nonsense restaurant serving some of the best udon in Kyoto. The adoration for this noodle spot means there are a lot more people that want to come here than there are seats, so you need to be strategic about arriving when it opens. You will be given a ticket and a designated time slot to return. The beef burdock udon is amazing.

🏠 34 Okazaki Minamigoshocho, Sakyo Ward

🚇 Higashiyama

📷 #yamamotomenzou

🕐 Fri – Thurs 11am – 6pm, Wed 11am – 2.30pm, Closed Thurs

🔔 No reservations, ticketing system

💲 ¥1,200

Giro Giro Hitoshina

8 *Kyoto Kaiseki*

Giro Giro Hitoshina is a creative kaiseki restaurant in a charming warehouse space overlooking the Takasegawa Canal. The traditional Japanese multi-course meal has been given a modern refresh here, toning down the usual formality to provide a fun and lighthearted dining experience. Request to sit at the 10-person counter and watch the vibrant chefs at work, crafting a delicious and delicate eight-course meal. The price is a very reasonable ¥4,200 for the set meal.

420-7, Matsubara Namba, Nishikiyacho

Kiyomizu-Gojo

+81 753437070

#girogirohitoshina

Mon – Sun 5.30pm – 11pm

Reservation by phone

¥4,200

Traveling Spoon

9 *Local Cooking Lesson*

⬈ travelingspoon.com

⊚ @travelingspoons

Ⓢ From ¥4,000

Traveling Spoon is a wonderful company set up by two female entrepreneurs in the US, with a mission to help travellers have meaningful and memorable cultural experiences through cooking with a local. In Kyoto, we went to the home of our host Keiko, where she welcomed us and helped us to prepare a traditional obanzai meal, which is native to the region. It's a fun and unique experience, spending quality time with a local in their home, chatting and learning about their culture through food.

⑩ Arashiyama Bamboo Grove

The bamboo grove at Arashiyama is one of the most famous sites in Kyoto and popular with tourists wanting to take a snap of the iconic landmark. It's best to visit early in the morning before the crowds descend with their selfie sticks. Arashiyama is about 9km west of Kyoto. Take the train from Kawaramachi Station in Kyoto to Arashiyama Station via Katsura.

⑪ Tenryuji Temple

While you're visiting the bamboo grove at Arashiyama, there are some lovely temples to combine your trip with, such as *Tenryuji* Zen temple. The temple's garden, *Sogenchi Garden* was laid out nearly seven hundred years ago by Zen master Muso Soseki. Enjoy the strolling pond garden, large standing rock arrangements and admire the use of 'shakkei' - borrowed scenery from the mountains.

🏠 68 Sagatenryuji Susukinobabacho, Ukyo Ward

🚇 Arashiyama Station

🏕 tenryuji.com

📷 #arashiyama

🕐 Arashiyama Bamboo Grove is always open; Tenryuji Temple is open from 8.30am – 5.30pm

💲 Free for Arashiyama Bamboo Grove; ¥500 for temple gardens

12 Sanjusangendo Temple

🏠 657 Sanjusangendomawari,
Higashiyama Ward

🚉 Shichijo

📍 sanjusangendo.jp

🕐 Mon – Sun 8am – 5pm
(April – Oct),
Mon – Sun 9am – 4pm
(Nov – March)

💲 ¥600

Sanjusangendo is a Buddhist temple founded in 1164 and famous for its 115m long hall with 1,001 statues, or 'kannons', made from wood and gold. The joint work of a team of 70, the sculptures are all similar but have slight differences in their facial expressions and lifelike hands. There's a wonderful international influence to some of the statues, including an Indian Garuda and an Ashura, the highest deity in Persia.

13 Murin-an

Murin-an is a modern Japanese garden, constructed in 1896, and a designated 'Place of Scenic Beauty'. It was built as the private residence of Yamagata Aritomo, a former Prime Minister and keen landscape designer. Master gardener Ogawa Jihee took a naturalist approach to its design, using the Higashiyama Mountains as a centre point and incorporating river streams using water from Lake Biwa.

🏠 31 Nanzenji Kusakawa-cho,
Sakyo Ward

🚉 Higashiyama

📍 murin-an.jp

📷 #murinan

🕐 Mon – Sun 9am – 6pm (Apr-Sept),
9am – 5pm (Oct – Mar)

💲 ¥410

Shisen-do Temple

14 *Tranquil Temple*

Temples in Kyoto fall into two camps: the wildly popular and crowded, such as *Fushimi Inari* in the centre of Kyoto, or quiet, serene and off-the-beaten-track sanctuaries such as *Shisen-do Temple*, located 9km north of Kyoto. *Shisen-do* was built as a hermitage in 1641 by Ishikawa Jozan, who was born into a samurai family and later became a scholar of Chinese poetry, calligraphy and landscape architecture. The small but atmospheric house and gardens have a distinctly warm and old-world feel, and you might find you're one of the only people here.

🏠 27 Ichijoji Monguchicho, Sakyo Ward

🚌 Take the number 5 bus from Kyoto to Ichijoji Sagarimatsucho

🏹 kyoto-shisendo.com

📷 #shisendotemple

🕐 Mon – Sun 9am – 5pm

💲 ¥500

Shugakuin Imperial Villa

15 *Scenic Site*

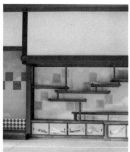

🏠 Shugakuin Yabusoe,
Sakyo Ward

🚉 Take the number 5 bus
from Kyoto to Shugakuin
Rikyudo Bus Stop

🏹 sankan.kunaicho.go.jp

📷 #shugakuin

🕐 Tues – Sun, Closed Mon

🔔 Reserve online or turn
up for the 1.30pm or
3pm tours

$ Free, but bring
your passport

A 20-minute walk from *Shisen-do Temple* is the stunning *Shugakuin Imperial Villa*. Set in an expansive 133-acre area at the foothills of the Higashiyama Mountains, this villa is a garden-lover's paradise, with its multiple layers of 'shakkei' – a technique by which gardens are designed to celebrate the backdrop landscape. Built by retired Emperor Gomizuno in 1659, it is styled as a 'detached palace', with villas and teahouses dotted on the lower, middle and upper gardens. We arrived in time for the 3pm guided tour, (the only way you can visit the villa).

Tofukuji Temple

16 *Meditative Moments*

Tofukiji is a Zen-Buddhist temple with a captivating Zen garden, and is one of my favourite places to visit in Kyoto. It was originally built in 1235, but has since been reconstructed due to fires, with some parts, such as the Sanmon gate, surviving from the 14th century. The 'Hojo' (Abbot's Hall) was rebuilt in 1890 and the surrounding gardens were designed in 1939 by landscape sculptor Mirei Shigemori. He devised four individual 'Hasso' gardens, a mix of traditional and abstract contemporary Zen gardens representing aspects of Buddha's life. The temple has a serene atmosphere and wasn't busy when we visited. The gardens are like remarkable living artworks, a truly meditative experience.

🏠 778 Honmachi, Higashiyama Ward

🚋 Tobakaido or Tofukuji

🔨 tofukuji.jp

📷 #tofukuji

🕐 Mon – Sun 9am – 4pm

💲 ¥400

Toji Temple Flea Market

17 *Quirky Curiosities*

There's a lovely local feel to the *Toji Temple Flea Market* – an event that occurs only on the 21st day of each month. We were in Kyoto on the 21st by chance so, on a cold, snowy February day, we cycled to the temple, which is just over 1km from Kyoto station. There's something for everyone at this market, from street food stalls selling hot taiyaki fish-shaped cakes to tables weighed down with piles of vintage kimonos. For ceramic fanatics, there's pottery galore, with gorgeous glazed pots and odd-shaped cups and vases on offer.

🏠 1 Kujocho, Minami Ward

🚃 Toji

🏹 toji.or.jp

📷 #tojitemplefleamarket

🕐 21st of each month, 6am – 4pm

195

Nara

In the 8th century **Nara** was the capital of Japan, a significant city steeped in cultural and historical importance and filled with prominent temples and art. Today these temples still stand, and the city is now well known for the deer that roam the region.

Getting there

The train takes 35 mins from Kyoto Station to Kintetsu-Nara Station or you can take the JR line to Nara Station using a JR pass.

18 Kofukuji National Treasure Museum

The *Kofukuji National Treasure Museum* displays the most beautiful Buddhist sculptures and artworks belonging to *Kofukuji Temple*, with pieces from Asuka, Nara, Heian, Kamakura, Muromachi, Momoyama and Edo throughout different periods of Japanese history. See the six-armed statue of Ashura and the rare lacquer statue of Garuda. The museum exhibits a range of artworks, from books, paintings and temple bells to gilt bronze lanterns.

⌂ 48 Noboriojicho, Nara

🚊 Nara

🏹 kohfukuji.com

🕐 Mon – Sun 9am – 5pm

$ ¥700

Todai-ji Temple

19 *Buddhist Wooden Wonder*

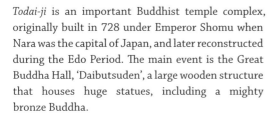

Todai-ji is an important Buddhist temple complex, originally built in 728 under Emperor Shomu when Nara was the capital of Japan, and later reconstructed during the Edo Period. The main event is the Great Buddha Hall, 'Daibutsuden', a large wooden structure that houses huge statues, including a mighty bronze Buddha.

🏠 406-1 Zoshicho, Nara

🚃 Nara

🏹 todaiji.or.jp

📷 #todaijitemple

🕐 Mon – Sun 8am – 5pm

💲 ¥600

20 Nara Deer Park

Located in central Nara, this park is as famous for the herds of deer that roam freely throughout as it is for its ancient temples. For many people, the deer are an attraction in themselves, and they are traditionally thought of as messengers of the gods in the Shinto religion.

⌂ Nara Park

🚆 Nara

21 Yoshiki-en Garden

Yoshiki-en is a small garden that is free for foreigners to visit, located between the *Todai-ji* and *Kofukuji* temples. The picturesque grounds include a pond garden, a moss garden and a thatched teahouse used for tea ceremonies.

⌂ 60-1 Noboriojicho, Nara

🚆 Nara

🕐 Mon – Sun 9am – 4.30pm

💲 Free for foreigners

22 Dormy Inn Umeda Higashi

We had one night in Osaka, a resting point after a full day of sightseeing in Nara and the starting point to our train journey to Mount Koya. *Dormy Inn* is a popular budget hotel chain, with branches all over Japan. Think of it as a Japanese version of Holiday Inn. The rooms are small, but the beds are super-comfortable and this one had a wonderful onsen.

🏠 3-5-3 5 Nishitenma, Kita Ward, Osaka

🚇 Minami-Morimachi

🏹 hotespa.net/dormyinn

$ From ¥8,000

23 Hozenji Sanpei

Come evening, the Dotonbori area of Osaka comes alive – a vibrant quarter with neon lights adorning every surface amid a hubbub of activity. I was initially on the search for takoyaki octopus balls, but was disappointed by the low-quality tourist offering. We then happily stumbled upon *Hozenji Sanpei*, an excellent okonomiyaki restaurant, where we sat at the counter and watched chefs create tasty savoury pancakes in front of us on a huge griddle.

🏠 1-7-10 Dotonbori, Chuo Ward, Osaka

🚇 Namba

⊘ Mon, Wed, Thurs, Fri 5pm – 11pm, Sat – Sun 11.30am –11pm, Closed Tues

🔔 Walk-in

$ ¥1,000

Mount Koya

Mount Koya, also known as 'Koyasan', is an elevated and secluded temple town 65km south of Osaka in Wakayama Prefecture. Established by Japanese Buddhist monk, Kobo Daishi, in 826 as the centre of Shingon Buddhist training, the area has hundreds of temples and monasteries, and for centuries has been part of an important pilgrimage route.

Getting there

From Osaka, go to Shin-Imamiya Station and take the Nankai-Limited Express to Gokurakubashi Station. From here, take the Nankai Koyasan Cable to Koyasan Station. The journey from Osaka to Koyasan takes around 2 hr 15 mins and costs ¥2,040 one-way.

24 Koyasan Zofukuin

For a unique experience, stay the night at a 'shukubo', a Buddhist temple providing lodging to guests run by monks. Shukubo were originally established as boarding for monks, but opened up as more pilgrims visited Mount Koya. *Zofukuin* is a traditional temple with simple accommodation set up for visitors. Rooms are Japanese-style, with tatami flooring and shared public baths. Dinner is served at 5.30pm; experience the Buddhist vegetarian cuisine 'shojin ryori', a traditional meal eaten by monks, which includes pickles, tofu, rice and soup dishes. At 6.30am guests are invited to join the Morning Prayer, a magical experience.

🏠 339 Koyasan, Koya

🚉 Koyasan

$ ¥20,000

Okunoin Cemetery

25 *Sacred Site*

🏠 Koyasan

🚊 Koyasan

📷 #okunoin

🕐 Mon – Sun 6am – 5.30pm
(Lantern Hall)

💲 Free

Okunoin Cemetery is the site of Kobo Daishi's mausoleum – an important destination for pilgrimages and one of the most sacred places in Japan. There are more than 200,000 tombstones and Buddhist memorials lining the path from Ichinohashi Bridge to the mausoleum, including those of prominent monks and well-known samurai lords. Walking along the path, you'll notice the five-tiered stupas, called 'Gorinto', which represent the five elements: earth, water, fire, wind and space. Enter the 'Torodo' Lantern Hall, a prayer chapel in front of the mausoleum, with 10,000 lanterns dedicated by worshippers that continuously burn today.

Kongobuji Temple

26 *Shingon Sanctuary*

Kongobuji is the head temple of Koyasan and Shingon Buddism. It was originally built in 1593 by Toyotomi Hideyoshi, and then rebuilt in 1863. It's a beautiful place to visit; you first enter a room called 'ohiroma', where you'll see beautiful sliding doors painted with Chinese-inspired gold cranes. Outside, there's the remarkable 'Banryutei', the largest rock garden in Japan that's designed to represent a pair of dragons emerging from a sea of clouds.

🏠 132 Koyasan

🚉 Koyasan

📷 #kongobuji

🕐 Mon – Sun 8.30am – 5.50pm

💲 ¥500

Reihokan Museum

27 *Koyasan Collection*

Reihokan Museum displays Buddhist art owned by the temples in Koyasan, with the aim of preserving the religious and cultural heritage of this sacred town. In Shingon Buddhism, works of art are especially important in the rituals, such as sounding instruments, incenses and ritual implements. The museum holds more than 28,000 objects that are 'National Treasures' or 'Important Cultural Properties', although only a select few items are exhibited at a time. See stunning pieces such as a silk scroll painting from the 10th-century Heian period and a Tang dynasty miniature Buddhist shrine dating from the 8th-century, which was brought back from China by Kobo Daishi.

🏠 306 Koyasan

🚌 Koyasan

⊘ Mon – Sun 8.30am – 5.30pm

$ ¥600

Tokyo's Tastiest Ramen

Words and photographs by Frank Striegl

Historically, ramen was 'borrowed' from neighbouring China. In the late 19th century, a large number of Chinese immigrants came to live and work in Japan, and they would regularly prepare various noodle dishes from home. Locals took notice of these dishes and were intrigued by their bold foreign flavours. Some took it upon themselves to tweak the recipes of these noodle dishes, which eventually led to the creation of the first shoyu (soy sauce) ramen. In 1910, shoyu ramen was first officially served at *Rairaiken*, a little eatery in Asakusa in north Tokyo.

Ramen is essentially noodles in hot soup, but it's also so much more. It has become an integral part of Japan's food soul and even its overall identity. More so than other foods in Japan, ramen speaks volumes about the ability of the Japanese to borrow something and, ultimately, perfect it.

Today, merely mentioning the word 'ramen' elicits such great excitement and unhinged, mouth-watering reactions from people. Patiently queuing for hours to eat piping hot ramen is no longer just a Japanese phenomenon. Ramen has dramatically taken the world by storm – and for excellent reason. Ramen is the ultimate soul food.

But ramen has come a long way from its humble 1910 beginnings. This magical dish is constantly evolving. New ramen styles and cooking techniques are born every year in Japan. Being Japan's capital and busiest city, Tokyo is at the centre of ramen's evolution. The variety and quality of ramen is astounding – we are simply spoiled for choice in Tokyo.

Types of ramen

There are countless varieties of ramen, especially if you look at them by region, from the heavy-hitting tonkotsu (pork bone) in Kyushu to the hearty miso ramen engineered to help battle the bitter winters in Sapporo city.

But, if we were to simplify things, there are four main types of ramen: **shoyu**, **shio**, **tonkotsu** and **miso**. Depending on the region or specific ramen shop, elements such as chicken, pork, vegetables and fish are used in the preparation.

Shoyu (soy sauce) is inherently important to Japanese cuisine, so it's fitting that the first ever ramen was made with shoyu seasoning. Shoyu ramen broth is brown, salty and tangy in flavour. Especially in Tokyo, curly noodles are normally used.

Shio literally means 'salt' and its clear broth is lighter, more bouncy and usually blended with plenty of vegetables. Noodles are often straight and not too thick.

Tonkotsu takes pork bones and boils them for hours and hours until they become part of a rich-tasting, milk-like broth. Thin straight noodles are very popular given tonkotsu ramen's history as a convenient, quick meal (thin noodles take less cooking time).

Miso (fermented soybean paste) ramen broth is rather heavy, thanks to a strong helping of pork lard. Thick, wavy noodles are the name of the game in miso ramen.

Kiraku

⌂ 2-17-6 Dogenzaka, Shibuya City

🚆 Shibuya

◷ Mon – Sun
11.30am – 8.30pm,
Closed Wed

$ ¥950

The ramen business is supremely competitive, with only a few ramen shops able to withstand the test of time. Kudos then to *Kiraku* in Shibuya, which has been standing strong since 1952. The hole-in-the-wall shop's interior isn't much to look at, but that's all part of the appeal. The bottom line is that the classic ramen served here has remained relevant for more than half a century. Its menu includes shoyu and shio options. Order 'Moyashi wantanmen', the shoyu ramen with beansprouts and dumplings; it's filling and full of a nostalgic flavour that's harder to come by these days. If you're feeling ambitious, order a side of their divine gyoza (fried dumplings) too.

Kinkatsu

⌂ 3-19-9 Toranomon, Minato City

🚆 Kamiyacho

◷ Mon – Fri 11am – 9.30pm,
Sat – Sun 11am – 6pm

$ ¥780

'Tantanmen' is a Sichuan-rooted ramen dish that features chilli oil, Sichuan pepper and sesame paste. Thanks to ramen shops like *Kinkatsu* who are redefining tantanmen, this dish is seeing a massive resurgence in popularity in Japan. *Kinkatsu's* modern tantanmen calls for more sesame seeds, which provides a creamier, nuttier taste. Its menu has several tantanmen variations – with soup, soupless (my preference) or even in tsukemen form. Each variation has a different level of spice using 'sansho' numbing peppers, ranging from one to three, although none are insanely spicy - allowing the sesame to properly stand out. Thick noodles perfectly soak up the smaller amount of spicy sesame broth.

Fuji Ramen

🏠 1-24-5 Asakusa,
Taito City

🚇 Asakusa

🕐 Mon – Sun
11am – 9pm

💲 ¥830

Asakusa is the birthplace of the first shoyu ramen shop in 1910, but that doesn't mean the local shops only serve this original style of ramen. *Fuji Ramen* focuses on a heavier tonkotsu shoyu ramen. This ramen is certainly heavier than the Asakusa standard, but it still doesn't weigh you down. *Fuji Ramen* has two types: tonkotsu shoyu or spicy miso, the second option being my recommendation – the tonkotsu base is still there, but the spicy miso makes the bowl come alive even more. *Fuji Ramen's* beautiful wooden countertops and handmade, medium-thick noodles are welcome bonuses.

Atariya Shokudo

🏠 215 Building, 2-15-3, Kanda Sudacho, Chiyoda City

🚇 Akihabara

🕐 Mon – Fri 11am – 3pm
and 7pm – 10pm,
Sat 11am – 8pm,
Closed Sun

💲 ¥700

Atariya Shokudo has been one of Akihabara's top ramen spots since entering the scene in 2011. It only has 15 seats, which – along with the shop's friendly owner, who spent years in the UK – makes for an intimate ramen experience. First-timers should order the 'Rairaimen', a Kyushu-inspired fusion that uniquely has a thick and starchy broth chock-full of vegetables like nira (garlic chives) and onions, minced pork and pillowy satsuma-age (fried fishcakes from Kagoshima). This thick broth comprises of chicken stock, a sweeter soy sauce from Miyazaki Prefecture, and zesty togarashi spice.

Tsukemen Gonokami Seisakusho

🏠 Chatelet Shinjuku Gyoen
Daichi Building 1F,
5-33-16 Sendagaya,
Shibuya City

🚇 Shinjuku

🕐 Mon – Sun
11am – 9pm

💲 ¥880

Tsukemen (dipping noodles) is basically deconstructed ramen, with the broth served separately from the noodles. This dish has actually been around since the 1950s, but there's since been much experimentation, with *Tsukemen Gonokami Seisakusho* a flag-bearer for the modern version. Its tsukemen is all about shrimp, and while the flagship shrimp tsukemen is undoubtedly delicious, I believe the better option is paired with tomato, the acidity of which brings down that salty shrimp taste. On top of the noodles, you'll find a side of pesto paste and even bread. Is this tsukemen or pasta? It doesn't matter – it's 2019 and it tastes so darn good.

Kamitoku

🏠 1-13-6 Ginza,
Chuo City

🚇 Ginza-itchome

🕐 Mon – Sun
11am – 10.30pm

💲 ¥650

Kamitoku specialises in a beef bone ramen that is out of this world. This version is less common as most ramen shops chiefly work with chicken and pork bones. *Kamitoku's* beefy broth is reminiscent of pho, but the marrowy richness from the beef bones provides a distinctly stronger flavour. As with a good steak, pepper is sprinkled throughout the bowl and does wonders for the overall taste. Mizuna vegetable toppings also provide a clean, refreshing crunch. *Kamitoku* is located in the glitzy Ginza area, but it is originally from Tottori Prefecture, the least populous of Japan's 47 prefectures. For a small-prefecture ramen shop, *Kamitoku* has done extremely well.

Kikanbo

🏠 2-10-9 Kajicho,
Chiyoda City

🚇 Kanda

🕐 Mon – Sat 11am – 9.30pm,
Sun 11am – 4pm

💲 ¥1,130

It's hard to put into words how much I love *Kikanbo*. Named after the iron club carried around by 'oni' (Japanese ogres), it is a pioneer in the 'umakara' (delicious and spicy) ramen space. Its miso ramen is a complex and careful blend of high-quality shinshu miso, premium pig and chicken bones, seafood, various vegetables, six kinds of red peppers and numbing pepper oil. Pictured is the miso ramen, which includes a massive piece of chashu pork and baby corn. At *Kikanbo*, you get to customise your spice and numbing pepper levels from one to five. Level one has none of either, while level five is 'oni' level – it's not for the faint of heart.

Tatsunoya

🏠 7-4-5 Nishishinjuku,
Shinjuku City

🚇 Shinjuku

🕐 Mon – Sun
11am – 11.30pm

💲 ¥850

No ramen shop list would be complete without a tonkotsu (pork bone) ramen, with *Tatsunoya* being one of the most popular spots not only in Shinjuku, but in all of Tokyo. *Tatsunoya* is from Kurume in Fukuoka Prefecture, the birthplace of tonkotsu ramen. Its ramen is rich but clean-tasting, and it proudly advertises the fact that its broth is 100% pork bone and cooked for a whopping 15 hours. Choose between the stronger flavour 'kokumi' or milder flavour 'junmi', my personal preference. The stronger flavour has more pork back fat, spicy miso and a silky oil made from garlic and burnt onions. You can't go wrong with either choice!

Ramen Housenka

🏠 1-24-6 Kabukicho,
Shinjuku City

🚆 Shinjuku

🕐 Mon – Sun
11.30am – 11.30pm

💲 ¥900

Capitalising on the recent trend of using tai (sea bream) fish bones, *Ramen Housenka* has been operating in the heart of crazy Kabukicho, Shinjuku, since July 2018. It does serve tsukemen, but be sure to order the ramen. Sea bream is a white fish with a milder taste. It therefore meshes well with *Housenka's* light shio seasoning. It's a deliciously fragrant bowl, topped off with seared sea bream and ultra-thin slices of roasted pork shoulder. Its transparent wheat noodles are no slouch either. This ramen bowl is ideal for those wanting to try artisan fish ramen without any overpoweringly sharp fish taste.

About the Author

Frank Striegl is a Filipino-American born in Tokyo and raised on ramen. He appropriately consumes more than 300 bowls of ramen a year, runs ramen-tasting tours in Tokyo at tokyoramentours.com and blogs at 5amramen. com. When he's not eating ramen, Frank enjoys reading, exercising and travel. He also is a huge 'Lord of the Rings' fan.

🏹 5amramen.com

📷 @5amramen

The Secret Sentos of Tokyo

Words and photographs by Stephanie Crohin

There's no better way to immerse yourself deeply into Japanese culture than by visiting a local bathhouse, called a 'sento', combining both cultural heritage and wellness that appeals to all the senses.

A sento is a public bathhouse, often run by a family, with their knowledge and expertise passed down through the generations.

Up until the mid-1950s, many Japanese people didn't have their own bath at home, so it was very common to visit the public baths on a daily basis.

Nowadays, most Japanese homes do have a bathroom, but there are still many reasons for visiting a sento. The functional element of washing the body is just one reason; in addition, people go for the relaxation benefits offered by the various large bathtubs, and to improve their overall health and beauty. Some visit a sento for the community aspects, and sometimes simply because of the beautiful bathhouse aesthetic.

The benefits of a sento are felt within the body and soul. They are like spas, each with its own unique history and charm. With numbers sadly declining every year, these days there are just over 500 bathhouses in Tokyo.

I suggest visiting a sento on the day of your arrival in Tokyo, to help you recover from travelling and to ease jet lag. Sentos are certainly a must-do during your trip; they are affordable mini paradises all around Japan.

Bathing Etiquette

Sento bathing requires a little familiarity with the rules and rituals:

- Leave your shoes in a locker at the entrance of the sento.

- Pay the bathing fee at the front desk. You can pay extra to borrow towels and for shampoo and soap. Sauna use requires an extra fee.

- Go to the changing room of your gender, undress and place your clothes and personal items in a locker. Leave the big towel in the locker and take the small towel with you for washing or drying after the baths.

- You enter the main bathing area naked (swimming costumes are not allowed). Men and women are in separate bathing areas.

- Next, enter the shower area. Tie up your hair if it's long. Sit down on a stool and wash your body with soap.

- Now you can enter the baths. Put your small towel on your head and be careful not to put it into the water.

- If you use the sauna, rinse your body in the shower area before entering the bath again.

- Don't hesitate to talk to people! The public bath is a space to share. People are very nice and you can easily communicate, even with only gestures if you don't speak Japanese.

Tattoos: Traditionally, public baths have prohibited those with tattoos, due to the link with organised crime. Sentos, on the other hand, mostly do allow tattoos (other super-sentos and onsens may have different rules). Note: All the sentos mentioned here accept tattoos.

Chiyo no Yu

🏠 Chiyonoyu Building,
1-4-31, Iguchi, Mitaka

🚌 Mitaka (take a bus
from Mitaka Station)

🕐 Mon – Fri
3.30pm – 11.30pm,
Sat – Sun
1pm –11.30pm

💲 ¥460. Sauna +¥200

With its air of tranquility, *Chiyo no Yu* has been an oasis in the city since 1965, located in Mitaka, in the west of Tokyo. There are two different bathrooms to discover, with access for men and women switching every two weeks. The outdoor area is amazing; one side is a Western-style garden, while the other is traditionally Japanese, and you can observe elements of each season in the surrounding nature. In May, for example, admire the purple wisteria ceiling hanging above the bath. There's also a view of the pond containing koi carp fish.

Matsu no Yu

🏠 6-23-15 Togoshi,
Shinagawa City

🚌 Nakanobu

🕐 Tues – Sat 3pm – 1am,
Sun 10am – 12am,
Closed Mon

💲 ¥460. Sauna +¥250

Three minutes' walk from Nakanobu Station in south Tokyo, you will find *Matsu no Yu*, opened in 1948. This is a cross between a traditional and a modern bathhouse, with the family who run it maintaining the original building and its old temple-style roof. *Matsu no Yu* is a real onsen, meaning the water is thermal and full of minerals. There is a Mount Fuji mural here painted by Morio Nakajima, one of the few painters left in Japan that preserve this unique mural art. *Matsu no Yu* has been used as a shoot location for many TV shows, most recently in the famous Japanese drama 'Doctor X'.

Okada-yu

🏠 3-43-2, Sekibara,
Adachi City

🚉 Nishiarai

🕐 Tues – Sun 3pm – 11.30pm,
Closed Mon

💲 ¥460. Sauna + ¥200
(steam sauna is free)

Run by the third generation of a family, *Okada-yu* is an elegant bathhouse nicknamed 'botanical sento' because of its amazing green paradise-like décor. The modern design of the space allows for lots of natural light and is decorated with many species of beautiful plants. There are different types of bath, including a 'hinoki' cypress wood bath, a cold bath, a nano-bubble bath, a sauna, a steam sauna and an outdoor bath in the men's bathroom. The water is soft, making it friendly to the skin. Afterwards, don't miss a visit to *Nishiarai Daishi*, a must-see temple only a few minutes' walk from there.

Yudonburi Sakaeyu

🏠 1-4-5 Nihonzutsumi,
Taito City

🚉 Minowa

🕐 Thurs, Fri, Sat, Mon and
Tues 2pm – 12am,
Sun 12pm – 12am,
Closed Wed

💲 ¥460. Sauna + ¥200

Centrally located close to Ueno and Asakusa, *Sakaeyu* is a hidden gem away from the nearby tourist crowds. *Sakaeyu* uses natural underground thermal water for its seven different types of baths. There's a large open-air bath, a nano-bubble bath and a one-person jar bath. In the sauna, there is pink Himalayan salt, which when diffused in the air is said to aid stress-relief. The outdoor bath is reminiscent of a ryokan-style setting, with a big bath surrounded by rocks and two smaller bowls inside it creating personal-sized mini baths. The outdoor bath is a micro-bubble bath that naturally cleanses the skin deeply. Water is warmed with solar panels.

Tsukimi-yu

⌂ 5-36-16, Akatsutsumi,
Setagaya City

🚃 Shimotakaido

🕐 Wed – Mon
3.30pm – 12am,
Closed Tues

Ⓢ ¥460. Sauna +¥240

Tsukimi-yu is a few minutes' walk from Shimotakaido Station, a charming residential area in Setagaya. *Tsukimi-yu* is a luminous blue sento with a mosaic-tiled wall meticulously depicting the classic image of Mount Fuji above the spacious baths. The onsen uses natural spring water, which warms the body deeply; it's particularly effective for stress relief and leaving the skin super-smooth and moisturised. There are various special massage baths here, such as the powerful jet-bath, a water-pressure massage and even the 'denkiburo' electric bath – a surprising experience in which a low-level electric current runs through the bath, which is meant to help with pain relief. The cold bath is great for increasing blood circulation.

Yoshi no Yu

⌂ 1-14-7, Naritahigashi,
Suginami City

🚃 Eifukucho or Shin-Koenji

🕐 Tues – Sun
1.30pm – 10pm,
Closed Mon

Ⓢ ¥460. Sauna +¥390

Located in west Tokyo, not far from Koenji, *Yoshi no Yu* is truly like a spa, with its various wellness baths to enjoy both inside and outside. The open-air carbonic spring bath is a must, with its sensation of being in a comfy cocoon. You can also experience Tokyo's unusual black onsen water, rich in minerals and known for its skin benefits. The sauna is spacious and even equipped with a TV. After the bath, enjoy local refreshments such as 'kakigori', a Japanese shaved-ice dessert topped with sweet flavoured syrup.

Akebono-yu

🏠 4-22-3 Adachi,
Adachi City

🚃 Gotanno

🕐 Fri – Wed 3pm – 12am,
Closed Thurs

Ⓢ ¥460. Sauna +¥200

It's hard not to love *Akebono-yu*, with its charming traditional building, retro changing rooms and marvellous mural art. Located a five-minute walk from Gotanno Station in north Tokyo, above the Arakawa River, the bath was constructed in 1957 and is carefully preserved by its third-generation owner. The wall painting in the women's baths is of Himeji Castle surrounded by sakura blossoms, while Mount Fuji decorates the men's bathroom. Outside, there's a small secret Japanese garden where you'll find a tranquil outdoor bath. Inside are several lovely baths – be sure to try the Chinese herbal one.

Fuku no Yu

🏠 5-41-5 Sendagi,
Bunkyo City

🚃 Honkomagome or Sendagi

🕐 Mon – Fri 11am – 12am,
Sat – Sun 8am – 12am

Ⓢ ¥460

Located in Sendagi in north Tokyo, *Fuku no Yu* was initially opened in 1972 and renovated in 2011 by Imai Kentaro, a renowned 'sento designer' architect who infuses a modern aesthetic with the aim of drawing young Tokyoites back to their local public baths. The interiors are bold and beautiful, mixing different styles of art; the traditional Mount Fuji paintings by mural experts Morio Nakajima and Kiyoto Maruyama are combined with modern graffiti-style artworks by local art-duo GravityFree who decorated the wooden wall partition. Special aromatic bath salts are regularly added to the water, creating funky colours and scents.

Fukumi-Yu

6-13-43 Kikuna,
Kohoku Ward,
Yokohama, Kanagawa

Kikuna

Tues – Sun 3pm –11.30pm,
Closed Mon

¥470. Sauna +¥200

Fukumi-Yu is a few minutes' walk from Kikuna Station, situated south of Tokyo on the way to Yokohama. The bathhouse was established in 1962 and the owner strives to maintain traditional customs, such as burning wood to heat the water – a method said to make the water softer. The mosaic mural of a mountain scene in the bathroom has been carefully preserved for 50 years, with the colours still bright and in good condition. Every Saturday, the owner prepares fresh lemon baths, with the mild citrusy perfume being particularly refreshing and relaxing.

About the Author

Stephanie Crohin was born in the south of France and, after initially coming to Japan as an exchange student in 2008, moved to Tokyo full-time in 2012 to work for a Japanese company. As a sento specialist, she works as an author, photographer and sento guide, and is an official sento ambassador for the Japan Association of Sento Culture. Stephanie loves to explore the public baths of Japan and has visited more than 800 sentos.

dokodemosento.com

@_stephaniemelanie_

Japan Photo Journal

Words and photographs by Kathryn Bagley

White Heron Dance

A participant in the White Heron Dance festival 'Shirasagi-no-Mai' takes a moment to show her wings individually and then bow to the temple at *Senso-ji*, Asakusa.

🏠 Senso-ji, 2 -3-1 Asakusa, Taito City, Tokyo

Sakura with blue gate

Two happy 'obaasan' (older ladies) sakura-gazing in Itabashi. On a beautiful sunny day, while exploring the Itabashi area's sakura bloom, I encountered these two elderly friends taking in the view.

 Itabashi, Itabashi City, Tokyo

Sakura Canal

Sakura in full bloom by the river near Waseda University. I encountered this view during a lovely long walk along the winding canal between Waseda and Iidabashi.

1-104 Totsukamachi, Shinjuku City, Tokyo

Sento with Mount Fuji mural

Tiled mural of Mount Fuji at *Magic Onsen Showa Bath*. Visiting retro Japanese sentos to take a communal soak and appreciate the beautiful design details is one of my top pastimes. This is my favourite Fuji mural in Tokyo because of its beautiful warm-toned gradients and ukiyo-e-style black outlines.

⌂ 3-30-1 Yushima, Bunko City, Tokyo

Japanese plum blossom over Mount Fuji

A Japanese plum blossom – or 'ume' – grove double-exposed over Mount Fuji in Odawara. Three hours west of Tokyo, there is a huge grove of plum trees at *Soga Bessho Bairin*, and on a clear day you can see Mount Fuji above the blossoms.

🏠 Soga Bessho Bairin, Odawara, Kanagawa

Indigo dyeing

Indigo dyeing at an atelier in Gujo Hachiman, Gifu. I visited the town of Gujo Hachiman for a work assignment documenting local specialties.

 Gujo Hachiman, Gifu Prefecture

Historic hearth

An antique iron kettle is heated by the 'irori', a traditional Japanese hearth at the *Edo-Tokyo Open Air Architectural Museum*. The museum is a goldmine for historic architecture and beautifully restored buildings that you can walk around.

 3-7-1 Sakuracho, Koganei, Tokyo

Autumn leaves

Changing seasons at *Edo-Tokyo Open Air Architectural Museum*. Being able to see and explore traditional thatched farmhouses within the metropolis of Tokyo is a really charming experience, and I always bring guests here for a day trip.

3-7-1 Sakuracho, Koganei, Tokyo

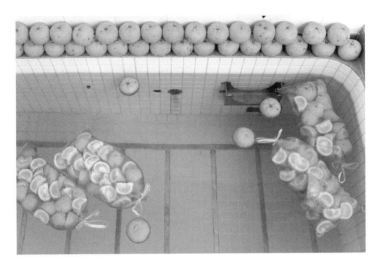

Yuzu bath

Fresh yuzu in the sento baths for winter solstice at *Kosugi-yu*, Koenji. These baths smelled absolutely amazing and it was wonderful to see and shoot a seasonal tradition meant to bring good health and good luck.

🏠 3-32-2 Koenjikita, Suginami City, Tokyo

Wagashi set

'Wagashi', Japanese tea sweets, themed for summertime. On my walks I love stopping into small local wagashi shops, such as *Baikatei* in Kagurazaka, to see what they have for the season.

 6-15 Kagurazaka, Shinjuku City, Tokyo

Japanese 'ume' plum blossom and bees

A bee drinks plum blossom nectar at *Yushima Tenjin*, a Shinto shrine in Bunkyo, Tokyo. I can't begin to describe how delicious the air smells during ume blossom season!

🏠 3-30-1 Yushima, Bunko City, Tokyo

Summer fireworks fan

Summer firework festival in Itabashi, Tokyo. Because of the humidity, summer nights tend to be pretty hot and stifling, so hand fans to cool off are a common sight.

 Itabashi, Itabashi City, Tokyo

Summer festival

Young girl tries her hand at the goldfish booth at a local festival, or 'matsuri', in Kagurazaka. Goldfish imagery is romanticised throughout Japanese art and on sartorial motifs.

Zenkokuji, 5-36 Kagurazaka, Shinjuku City, Tokyo

Izakaya exterior

Restaurant, or 'izakaya', exterior at dusk in Arakawa. This scene encapsulates for me how it feels to walk around 'real' Tokyo – it's the quintessential traditional ma-and-pop shopfront aesthetic.

 Machiya Station, Arakawa, Tokyo

About the Photographer

 Kathryn Bagley is an American photographer based in Tokyo. She has lived in the city for five years and falls more in love with it every day. Before moving to Japan, she lived in New York City and shot primarily wedding and engagement portraits. Since living in Japan, she has been so inspired by the culture and history that she has segued into shooting local festivals and historic areas of note.

 kitsunephoto.squarespace.com

@kitsunekun

Tokyo Index

Accommodation	Type	Page
Airbnb	*Apartment*	23
Claska	*Hotel*	20
Hoshinoya Tokyo	*Ryokan*	22
Hyatt Centric Ginza	*Hotel*	21
Muji Ginza	*Hotel*	19
Nohga Hotel Ueno	*Hotel*	20
The Millennials Shibuya	*Capsule Hotel*	18

Lunch

	Type	Page
Abe	*Sushi*	66
Afuri	*Ramen*	30
Aoyama Flower Market	*Cafe*	95
Bio Ojiyan Cafe	*Cafe*	111
Butagumi	*Tonkatsu*	96
Ginza Kagari Honten	*Ramen*	139
Golden Brown	*Burger*	52
Henry's Burger	*Burger*	33
Higashi-yama	*Modern Japanese*	54
Hiroki	*Okonomiyaki*	110
Inshotei	*Kaiseki*	152
Menya Nukaji	*Ramen*	31
Pizza Slice	*Pizza*	101
Seirinkan	*Pizza*	53
Shuichi	*Ramen*	31
Standing Sushi Bar	*Sushi*	124
Sushi No Midori	*Sushi*	66
Tonkatsu Suzuki	*Tonkatsu*	138
Trasparente	*Bakery*	50
Tsujihan	*Kaisendon*	139
Tsukiji Market	*Seafood*	146
Uoriki Kaisen Sushi	*Sushi*	32

Many places for lunch are also open for dinner.

Coffee

	Type	Page
Bear Pond Espresso	*Coffee*	112
Café Kitsuné	*Coffee*	94
Onibus Coffee	*Coffee*	51
Sidewalk Stand	*Coffee*	51

Sweets

Good Town Doughnuts	*Doughnuts*	80
Mister Donut	*Doughnuts*	124
Nico Donuts	*Doughnuts*	67
Naniwaya Sohonten	*Taiyaki*	67

Dinner

Cignale Enoteca	*Italian-Japanese*	35
Falò	*Italian-Japanese*	37
Hiroo Onogi	*Modern Japanese*	36
Kyubey	*Sushi*	140
Nobu	*Sushi*	70
Shirosaka	*Modern Kaiseki*	69
Sushi Harumi	*Sushi*	141
Taku	*Sushi*	100
Ushigoro S	*Yakiniku*	98
Yoroniku	*Yakiniku*	99

Casual Dinner

Kaikaya by the Sea	*Izakaya / Seafood*	34
KushiWakaMaru	*Yakitori*	55
Savoy	*Pizza*	68
Shinjuku Omoide Yokocho	*Yakitori*	125
Tonkatsu Tonki	*Tonkatsu*	56
Toriyoshi	*Yakitori*	97

Bar	Type	Page
Cote D'Azur	*Karaoke*	74
Golden Gai	*Casual*	127
Little Smith	*Cocktails*	142
New York Bar	*Cocktails*	126
Shibuya Nonbei Yokocho	*Casual*	38

Shop		
85 / Hachigo	*Deli & Homeware*	57
Beams	*Clothing*	128
Champion	*Clothing*	85
Chicago	*Vintage Clothing*	86
Daikanyama T-Site	*Books & Magazines*	41
Deus Ex Machina	*Lifestyle /Clothing*	84
Disk Union	*Vinyl*	42
Dover Street Market	*Clothing*	143
Farmer's Market @ UNU	*Food Market*	104
Flamingo	*Vintage Clothing*	113
Fog Linen Work	*Homeware / Lifestyle*	117
Found Muji	*Homeware*	102
H Beauty & Youth	*Clothing*	101
Haight & Ashbury	*Vintage Clothing*	114
Hareginomarusho	*Kimono*	118
Isetan	*Department Store*	129
Issey Miyake	*Clothing*	103
J'antiques	*Vintage Clothing*	59
Kalma	*Vintage Clothing*	116
Konguri	*Vintage Homeware*	60
Muji	*Clothes & Homeware*	39
Oedo Antique Market	*Secondhand Market*	144
Ohya Shobo	*Antique Books*	156
Opening Ceremony	*Clothing*	83
Oriental Bazaar	*Souvenirs*	81
Tokyo Edo Miso	*Miso Paste*	40
Toll Free	*Vintage Clothing*	60
Traveler's Factory	*Stationery*	58
Tsutaya Roppongi	*Bookshop & Cafe*	71

Shop	Type	Page
United Arrows	*Clothing*	82
We Go	*Vintage Clothing*	115
Yoyogi Park Flea Market	*Secondhand Market*	88

Sights & Museums

21_21 Design Sight	*Art Museum*	72
Edo-Tokyo Museum	*Museum*	157
Hamarikyu Gardens	*Park*	145
Japan Open-Air Folk House Museum	*Museum*	119
Kyu Asakura House	*House & Garden*	43
Mori Art Museum	*Art Museum*	73
Nanzuka	*Art Gallery*	44
Nezu Museum	*Art Museum*	105
Ota Memorial Museum of Art	*Art Museum*	87
Ryogoku Kokugikan	*Sumo Stadium*	158
Samurai Museum	*Museum*	132
Shibuya Crossing	*Sight*	45
Shinjuku Gyoen National Garden	*Park*	131
Sogetsu School of Ikebana	*Ikebana Class*	75
Tokyo City View	*View Point*	73
Tokyo National Museum	*Museum*	153
Yayoi Kusama Museum	*Art Museum*	133
Yoyogi Park & Meiji Shrine	*Park*	89

Public Bath

Edoyu	*Sento*	155
Haginoyu	*Sento*	155
Kohmeisen Sento	*Sento*	61
Maenohara Onsen Sayano Yudokoro	*Sento*	154
Thermae-Yu	*Sento*	130

Behind the Scenes

A few photos taken during my trips to Japan.

Golden Brown, Tokyo

Hoshinoya Fuji, Mount Fuji

Tokyo Metro

Hotel Kamon, Hakone

Shinjuku Omoide Yokocho, Tokyo

Hozenji Sanpei, Osaka

Afuri, Tokyo

Yayoi Kusama Museum, Tokyo

Shugakuin Imperial Villa, Kyoto

Sushi Harumi, Tokyo

Hakuba

Oedo Antique Market, Tokyo

Cote D'Azur, Tokyo

My Tokyo & Beyond Travel Notes

Date   Location   Notes

Lost Guides Books

Also available
in the Lost Guides
Travel Series:

Lost Guides – Bali & Islands
ISBN 978-981-11-4361-8

Lost Guides – Singapore
ISBN 978-981-11-1909-5

Acknowledgements

Thank you to all those that joined me in Japan for the exploration side of the project, as well as those that gave me their tips and shared their secrets from Tokyo and beyond with me.

A big thank you to the team that helped me to produce this book, my designers Sarah and Schooling, editor Rebecca Dyer and illustrator Rinanda Adelia. Thank you to the people who contributed their Tokyo expertise - Frank Striegl, Stephanie Crohin, Kathryn Bagley and Danielle Demetriou.

Additional photography:

The Millennials Shibuya
Muji Hotel Ginza
Nohga Hotel Ueno
Claska
Kohmeisen Sento
Ota Memorial Museum of Art
Thermae-Yu
Maenohara Onsen Sayano Yudokoro
Haginoyu
Edoyu
Owakudani
Malda Kyoto
Kofukuji National Treasure Museum
Dormy Inn
Reihokan Museum
Kathryn Bagley - Juri Nagai